New Mexico Treasure Tales

OTHER CAXTON BOOKS
BY W. C. JAMESON

Colorado Treasure Tales
ISBN 0-87004-402-8
6x9, 208 pages, paper $13.95

NEW MEXICO TREASURE TALES

W. C. Jameson

CAXTON PRESS
Caldwell, Idaho
2003

© 2003 by W. C. Jameson

Library of Congress Cataloging-in-Publication Data

Jameson, W. C., 1942-
  New Mexico treasure tales / by W.C. Jameson.
    p. cm.
  ISBN 0-87004-429-X
  1. New Mexico--History, Local--Anecdotes. 2. Treasure-trove--New Mexico--Anecdotes. 3. New Mexico--Antiquities--Anecdotes. 4. Gold mines and mining--New Mexico--History--Anecdotes. 5. Silver mines and mining--New Mexico--History--Anecdotes. 6. Outlaws--New Mexico--History--Anecdotes. I. Title.
  F796.6.J36 2003
  978.9--dc21   2003001163

Lithographed and bound in the United States of America
CAXTON PRESS
Caldwell, Idaho
169308

New Mexico, 1895

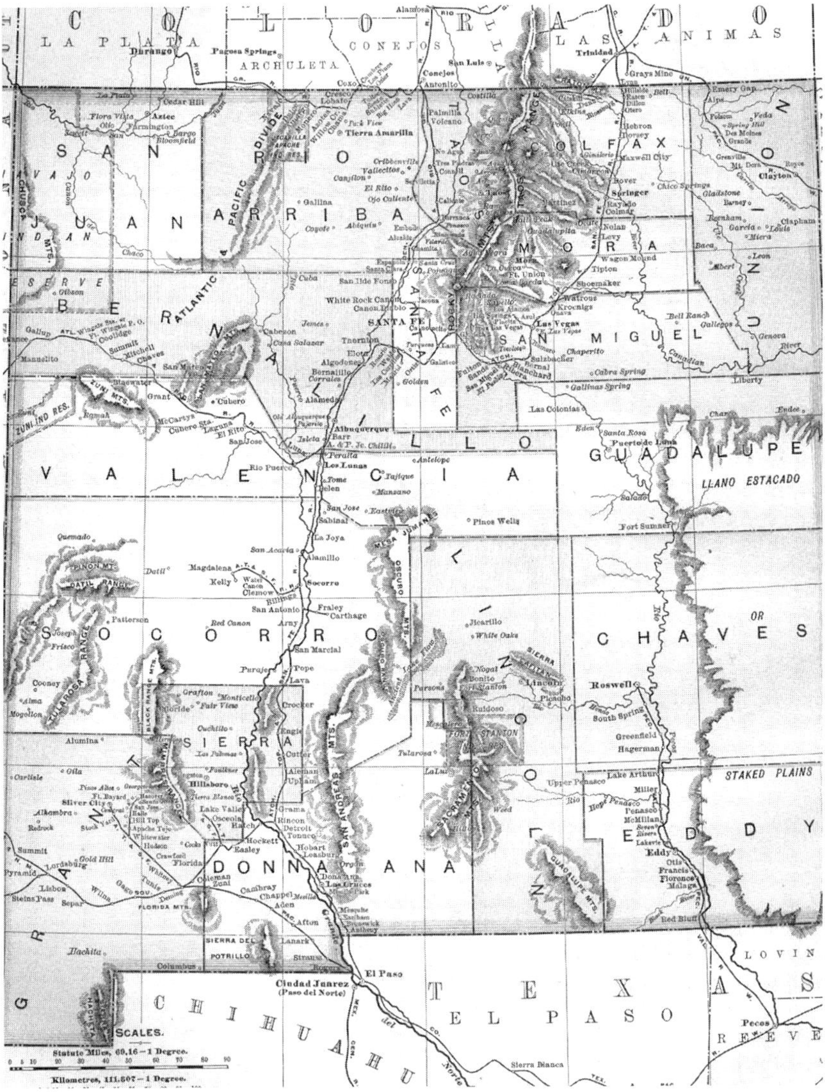

COLORADO
LA PLATA
ARCHULETA
CONEJOS
LAS ANIMAS
Durango
Pagosa Springs
Trinidad
San Luis
SAN JUAN
RIO ARRIBA
TAOS
COLFAX
MORA
UNION
Aztec
Farmington
Tierra Amarilla
Springer
Clayton
BERNALILLO
SANTA FE
SAN MIGUEL
SANTA FE
Las Vegas
VALENCIA
Albuquerque
Los Lunas
GUADALUPE
Puerto de Luna
Santa Rosa
LLANO ESTACADO
Fort Sumner
SOCORRO
Socorro
San Marcial
Magdalena
LINCOLN
Lincoln
White Oaks
CHAVES
Roswell
SIERRA
Hillsboro
GRANT
Silver City
Lordsburg
Deming
DONNA ANA
Las Cruces
EDDY
Eddy
STAKED PLAINS
El Paso
Ciudad Juarez
(Paso del Norte)
TEXAS
EL PASO
REEVES
LOVING
CHIHUAHUA
SCALES.
Statute Miles, 69.16 = 1 Degree.
Kilometres, 111.307 = 1 Degree.

CONTENTS

MAPS

INTRODUCTION

New Mexico.

The Land of Enchantment!

And enchanting it is in so many ways. This compelling land of magic and mystery offers enchanting vistas of mountains and desert, canyon and plain. Here one finds slopes for skiing, rivers for floating, trails for exploring, great cities for adventure, and small towns for relaxing. But in New Mexico, one finds more, much more.

In addition to all of these natural and varied settings, New Mexico claims a history unlike that of any of the other grand united states, one filled with characters from myriad cultures along with dramatic, compelling, and colorful events generating an edge-of-your-seat kind of excitement.

And as if all of the above were not enough, the state of New Mexico has given birth to some of the most amazing and incredible legends and tales of lost mines and buried treasures.

The Physical Setting

Few states rival New Mexico for sheer physical beauty. Majestic mountain peaks rising above the plain kiss the cerulean sky, peaks formed and shaped and sculpted by natural events both violent and subtle, geologic events that have been ongoing for millions of years, events that continue today.

During the previous millennia, great stresses in the earth's crust squeezed, folded, and uplifted huge portions of the landscape to form the Rocky Mountains that stretch from Alaska southward into Mexico, a range that runs the north-south length of New Mexico. Once these mountains were pushed thousands of feet above the ground, the erosional effects of glaciers, flowing water, wind, gravity, and time began to do their work, ultimately carving, molding, and sculpting the rugged features that greet us today as we drive through this magnificent scenery.

Over time, the mountains were shaped into their distinctive peaks, sharp-edged ridges, and shaded canyons. The weathered and eroded debris from the higher elevations were carried downslope, across vast distances, and ultimately deposited along watercourses such as the Rio Grande, the Gila, the Pecos, and the Canadian to form vast, fertile floodplains.

Here and there, the weathering and erosion of the great outcrops of granite exposed rich deposits of gold, silver, and other minerals, many of which eventually became so very important to the people who sought to conquer and colonize this wild, rugged land and its natives. Many of the stories related to the search for and the mining and transportation of these valuable minerals have entered the rich realm of legend and folklore. A number of these original deposits, lost over time, are still searched for today. Some are occasionally rediscovered.

The Cultural Setting

The first people to settle in what was eventually to become the state of New Mexico were early American Indians, mostly hunters and gatherers who went about the daily business of survival long before the horse was introduced into the region by the Spaniards. Numerous manifestations of their culture have been discovered and studied and have enriched our knowledge of these prehistoric tribes.

Many of these early Indian occupants became successful farmers, as their sophisticated irrigation channels and bounty of crops testify. Architecturally, they were fascinating and inventive to the point of being functionally artistic as manifested by the rock dwellings found at Chaco Canyon, Acoma Pueblo, Gila Cliff Dwellings, and other locations. Though the idea remains controversial, scientists tell us that the survival of these early New Mexico residents was eventually threatened by a prolonged drought which forced them to pack up and abandon the region.

In the sixteenth century, newcomers arrived in New Mexico that were to forever change the culture and activities of the region. Mounted and armed Spaniards came with a mission: Sent by the government and the church in their homeland, the Spanish set about exploring much of the American West, inventorying the cultures found within, and examining the potential of establishing trade, agriculture, and commerce. Additionally, the Spaniards were charged with the responsibility of prospecting for rich deposits of ore which were to be mined, processed, and shipped across the Atlantic Ocean to fill the treasuries of Spain.

And find the ore they did. Hundreds of mines were developed, mines which yielded ton after ton of gold and silver. Uncountable fortunes were transported back to Mexico, loaded onto ships at the gulf ports, and carried across the wide sea to Spain. Many of these treasure-filled vessels were lost to the bottom of the Atlantic as a result of violent storms. Millions more in gold and silver were lost during the transport across the land via wagon and pack train as a result of attack by Indians and bandits.

Some of this wealth was eventually recovered, but much of it remains lost to this day.

In 1680, the Pueblo Indians, hundreds of whom were enslaved by the Spanish and forced to labor in the mines, rebelled, armed themselves, and rode throughout the area wreaking revenge on all the Spaniards they encountered, revenge for the numerous injustices they suffered.

Just prior to fleeing the area, officials ordered the closing of all the mines and instructed they be covered over to hide them from the Indians. The Spanish believed that, in time, they would return to the area, reclaim their authority, and resume excavation.

In some cases this eventually came about, in others, the mines remained lost, even to this day.

During the eighteenth century, the territory that was to become the state of New Mexico was visited often by explorers, trappers, prospectors, and those interested in the possibilities of settlement, of establishing farms and ranches and business enterprises.

During this time, even more discoveries of gold and silver were made, more riches dug from the mountainsides, and men became wealthy. Towns and cities were established and grew and bustling commerce evolved. All of this progress was soon followed by a breed of men who saw opportunities to become rich from the labors of others. Outlaws arrived in the area to rob the gold and silver ore and ingots as well as payrolls from the trains, from the stagecoaches, from the hapless miners who offered little in the way of defense. Outlaw loot was sometimes hidden, the outlaws subsequently captured and/or killed and never able to return to reclaim their booty. Numerous sites of lost and buried outlaw gold still exist throughout New Mexico.

The Tales

New Mexico is incredibly rich in legend and folklore, particularly as it relates to tales of lost mines and buried treasures. There are some who would argue that New Mexico is the location for some of the largest natural deposits of lost gold and silver in the nation. Others claim that many of the the most mysterious and compelling tales of hidden treasures can be found here. Indeed, a few have been.

The legends and tales of lost mines and buried treasures presented in this book are the result of over four decades of search, research, exploration, and discovery. In some cases, treasure was found and recovered and lost mines reopened and reentered for the first time in over 300 years. Using the available evidence, professional and amateur treasure hunters continue to search for lost and buried outlaw loot.

For reasons related to the organization and presentation found in this book, the state of New Mexico has been divided into four unequal sections–Northwest, Northeast, Southeast, and Southwest—as a result of two dominant features—The Rio Grande and Interstate 40. The Rio Grande conveniently flows from north to south in a slightly meandering channel, conveniently bisecting the state in a ragged line. Interstate 40, a man-made feature running east-west, cuts the state into northern and a southern portions. Since these features are generally referred to by residents when providing directions, they will suit us just fine for establishing somewhat unequal yet efficiently delineated regions of concentration.

Since I was a young man of twenty, I have spent countless hours roaming and exploring the remote regions of

New Mexico in search of lost mines and buried treasure. Just as importantly, I diligently pursued the search for the stories, the legends, which aroused so much interest and excitement among men who dream of wealth. I worked at separating fact from fiction and prowled libraries and old journals and diaries in search of corroborating evidence.

In chasing down the history and, hopefully, the truth, I was privileged to meet and visit with New Mexicans from all walks of life: Cowhands, farmers, postmasters of small towns, bankers, newspapermen, and others, all of whom contributed their knowledge of the history and culture. I interviewed men and women who spent years searching for some of these treasures, I spoke with some who actually found lost gold. I spoke with descendants of some of the principal characters in these tales.

In the end, I came away with an intense appreciation for the folk, for the land, and for the rich cultural heritage of New Mexico.

I now invite the reader to enter this amazing and mysterious world of New Mexico's lost mines and buried treasures, to travel with me from region to region and become immersed in the fascinating stories.

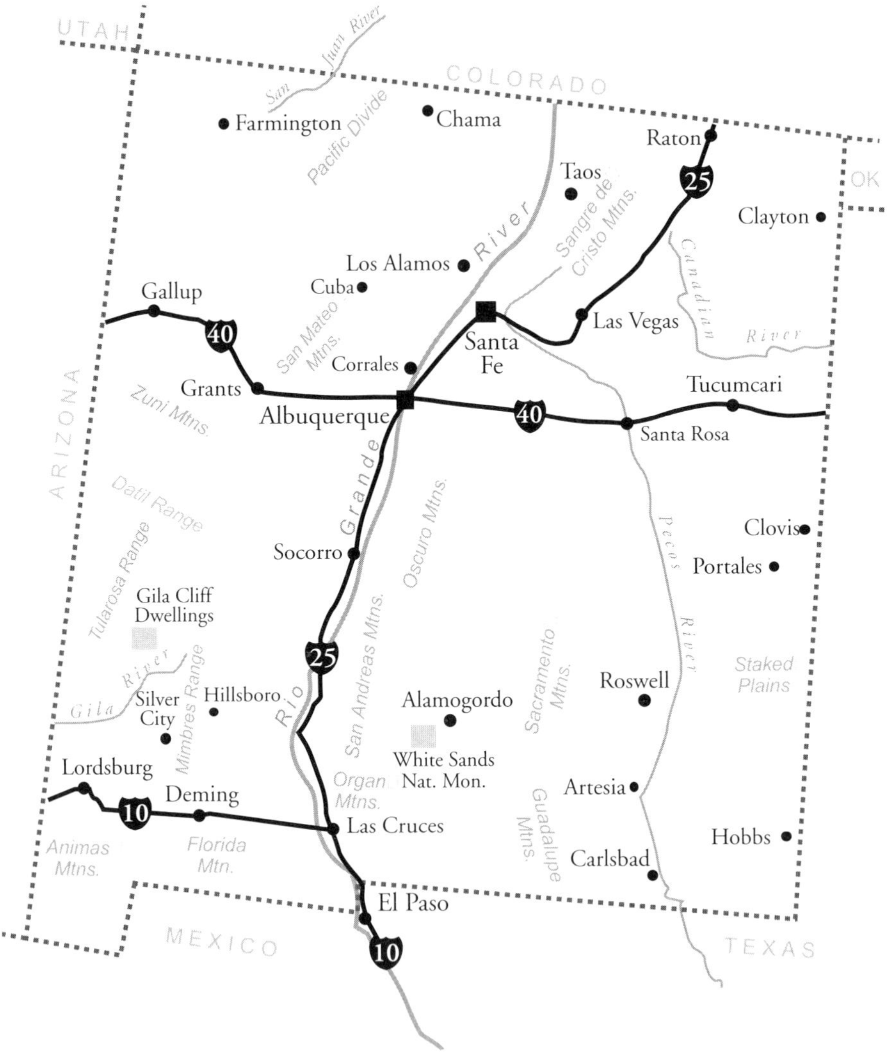
UTAH
COLORADO
OK
ARIZONA
MEXICO
TEXAS
San Juan River
Pacific Divide
Farmington
Chama
Raton
Taos
Sangre de Cristo Mtns.
Clayton
Canadian River
Los Alamos
Rio Grande River
Cuba
Gallup
Santa Fe
Las Vegas
San Mateo Mtns.
Corrales
Grants
Albuquerque
Tucumcari
Santa Rosa
Zuni Mtns.
Datil Range
Oscuro Mtns.
Pecos River
Clovis
Portales
Socorro
Tularosa Range
Gila Cliff Dwellings
San Andreas Mtns.
Sacramento Mtns.
Staked Plains
Gila River
Silver City
Mimbres Range
Hillsboro
Alamogordo
Roswell
White Sands Nat. Mon.
Lordsburg
Deming
Organ Mtns.
Artesia
Guadalupe Mtns.
Las Cruces
Hobbs
Animas Mtns.
Florida Mtn.
Carlsbad
El Paso
25
40
10

NORTHWEST

THE LOST CANCINO ARROYO TREASURE

Tres Piedras is a small village located in north-central New Mexico some twenty-five miles west of the Rio Grande. A number of deep, water-carved gullies in this region called arroyos lead to the historic river, their ephemeral waters a result of the occasional rains that bring life-giving moisture to this otherwise arid environment. When there is no rain, as is the case throughout most of the year, these stream beds remain dry.

One such drainage channel is called Cancino Arroyo, a winding, sometimes deep gully located between Tres Piedras and the Rio Grande in Rio Arriba County. Local legend offers that dozens of solid gold ingots believed to be worth well over one million dollars in today's values lie buried under several feet of sand and gravel at the bottom of this arroyo. There are a handful of elderly residents that live in this area who claim to know the exact location of the gold, but over a century of erosion and deposition, coupled with the soft and porous bottom of the arroyo, has hampered a number of recovery operations.

All who have researched this amazing tale are convinced the gold is still there, still buried in the sands at the bottom of Cancino Arroyo.

* * *

The story involving the Cancino Arroyo gold began unfolding on August 9, 1880 in Cimarron, New Mexico, a growing community located some sixty miles east of Tres Piedras. Porter Stockton, along with a companion named West, became embroiled in a dispute which ended in a gunfight. Stockton, a local outlaw with a reputation for robbery and murder, killed two men in a matter of seconds. He and West immediately mounted their horses and fled westward to their hideout in Gallegos Canyon not far from Tres Piedras.

The two outlaws crossed the Rio Grande around midday, and after reaching the west bank they noticed storm clouds forming in the northwest. Moments later, a light rain began falling. During the next hour, however, the rain grew heavier, making travel quite difficult. By evening, a raging storm brought dense rainfall which reduced visibility to only a few feet. Much of the trail was washed out, and soon the two men found themselves lost.

Inadvertently, Stockton and his partner rode into a deep arroyo and followed its course, hoping it would lead to higher ground and an opportunity to recognize familiar landmarks.

Unknown to the two outlaws, a party of three men were approximately one-half hour behind them on the same trail. Like Stockton, the three were also lost in the storm and had turned into the same arroyo in the hope of getting their bearings. Trailing along on lead ropes just behind the three men were two stout, heavily-laden mules, each carrying a fortune in gold ingots in leather packs. A few weeks earlier, these same travelers followed the directions they had interpreted from a very old and faded parchment map and found a large cache of Spanish gold, long-hidden in an abandoned mine shaft far to the southwest in Arizona. After loading as many ingots as their leather panniers could accommodate, the three set out on the long journey to their homes in Colorado where they intended to sell the treasure and make plans to return to the cache and retrieve the remaining gold. They were less than 100 miles from their destination when they were caught in the heavy storm.

Since they had never before visited this part of New Mexico, the newcomers became confused and disoriented when the trail they were following was washed away. Spotting the tracks of the two riders who passed this way a short time earlier and believing they must be familiar with the terrain, the trio turned into the arroyo and followed them.

As Stockton and West traveled up the arroyo, they noted that it grew deeper, the vertical walls stretching sixty to seventy feet high in placess. The normally dry stream bed had become a surging sand- and silt-laden flow that was nearly one-foot deep. Noting that the current was getting stronger, the water rising, and the bottom sands turning soft and threatening, Stockton suggested a return to the opening of the arroyo and a search for a more acceptable route. As the two men retraced their path occasional flashes of lightning illuminated the walls of the gully.

On rounding a sharp bend in the channel, Stockton and West came face to face with the three riders advancing up the arroyo. Stockton immediately assumed the three were part of a posse sent out to capture or kill them, and at the next lightning flash he pulled his revolver from its holster and fired, charging into the riders as he did so. Right behind him came West.

The surprise attack rendered the three riders stunned and helpless. Before they could regain their composure, all were lying dead, their bodies partially covered by the rising water of the arroyo. Stockton and West also shot and killed the three horses and two mules, then fled as fast as their horses could carry them toward the mouth of the arroyo and thence to Gallegos Canyon.

Stockton and West, mistaking the three horsemen for lawmen, were completely unaware they had just ridden away from a fortune in gold ingots.

As the outlaws fled toward their hideout, the heavy rain continued to fall and dense sheets of runoff from the slopes of the nearby mountains flowed into the numerous channels which fed the Rio Grande. Approximately one hour after the killing of the three men, Cancino Arroyo was inundated with a raging flash flood several feet deep. The waters, carrying a heavy load of sediment, washed over the dead men and horses.

In the sunshine and cleansed air of the following morning, two Mexican sheepherders—and old man and a young boy—awoke from their storm-tossed sleep. The temporary lean-to fashioned from limbs and grasses afforded little protection from the wind and downpour of the previous night. As the old man looked over the herd of some seventy sheep that was in his care, he remarked to the youngster that he thought he heard gunshots sometime in the night.

After determining that none of the sheep were missing, the old herder walked the few yards to rim of Cancino Arroyo and looked into the deep, shadowed channel. Several inches of water still flowed along the sandy bottom, and as his old eyes grew accustomed to the morning shadows below, the sheepherder spotted what he thought were the bodies of three men and the carcasses of several horses. Summoning the boy, the two scrambled down the steep bank of the arroyo and came upon the grisly scene. Cutting open one of the leather packs, the sheepherder withdrew an eighteen-inch-long object that he believed to be a piece of iron. Curious, he sliced open the remaining packs only to find more of the same. Having no need of the metal, the herder simply tossed the ingots on the ground.

Finding nothing of value, the herder and the boy climbed back to the rim of the arroyo and returned to the job of caring for the flock of sheep. The old man had kept one of the ingots, and as he passed the rude lean-to, he tossed it inside among his few belongings.

Later that afternoon, the rains came again, this time lighter than the day before but lasting well into the night. That evening as the two sheepherders attempted to keep dry under their flimsy lean-to, Cancino Arroyo accommodated yet another flash flood, this one with waters nearly ten feet deep, waters that raced and crashed along the bottom and swept away everything in their path.

Late the following morning, Dolores Cancino, a rancher and the owner of the sheep in the care of the old man and the boy, arrived with supplies for his herders. As he unloaded food and other items, the old herder told his employer of what he found in the arroyo. When finished, the herder handed Cancino the bar he retrieved from the leather pack. Cancino hefted the ingot and scraped away at its surface with a tough thumbnail. A look of surprise washed over him as he recognized the object as being composed of almost pure gold!

Assigning the lad to watch over the sheep, Cancino and the old herder returned to the bottom of the arroyo. Wading through two-feet deep water, they dug at the mud in an attempt to locate the bodies of the men and animals and gold, but were unable to find anything. Returning to the top, Cancino elected to spend the night at the camp and examine the arroyo the next morning when he was certain the flow would have ceased.

Shortly after sunrise, Cancino and the old man were back in the arroyo, probing and digging in the sands but finding nothing. After determining that the surging waters of the flash flood must have carried men, animals, and gold downstream, Cancino rode his horse along the rim of the canyon searching the streambed for some sign. Finally, after traveling several dozen yards he spotted one of the dead horses partially buried in the sands. After finding a route to the bottom, Cancino located two more horses and one mule. The bodies of the three men were nowhere to be seen and none of the gold was apparent.

One week later, Cancino rode south to Santa Fe where he asked a friend to assay the ingot. The report stated that it was composed of a high grade of gold and cast in the manner of the early Spanish miners. The assayer paid Cancino over $2,000 for the bar.

During the following months, Cancino explored up and down the bottom of the arroyo that bore his name but still found nothing. When the rains came and the runoff flooded through the arroyo, Cancino would hurry to the location in the hope that the most recent surge of current might have uncovered some of the gold, but he had no luck.

In September 1881, Cancino became acquainted with a man named Steve Upholt, an experienced miner. Reluctantly, he told Upholt about the gold bars be believed to be lying scattered somewhere along the bed of Cancino Arroyo. Upholt surprised Cancino by telling him that the gold was very likely in the same place where it was originally dumped from the panniers and that it had undoubtedly sunk several inches to several feet into the soft and yielding bottom sands of the arroyo. Upholt explained that when sand becomes saturated with water it becomes unstable and turns into quicksand. Anything heavy, such as a gold bar, would almost immediately sink to some depth below the surface.

Cancino and Upholt decided to form a partnership and search for the gold together. Almost two months later, Upholt arrived at the sheep camp near the rim of Cancino

Arroyo and spent several days exploring up and down the stream bed. Since the three unknown riders were killed and the gold dumped out, a number of flash floods tearing through the narrow channel created changes in the arroyo. Deposition of water-borne sands had filled the bottom and portions of the walls had caved in, all leading Upholt to believe the gold would be found much deeper than he originally believed. To add to the difficulty of recovery, the configuration of the channel had changed so much that the old sheepherder could not be certain of the exact location of his original discovery of the bodies and the gold.

One afternoon many weeks later while walking along the arroyo bottom, Upholt chanced upon a human skeleton, the gleaming white bones partially exposed. After scraping away the covering sand, he found some rotted clothes and boots still clinging to the frame. Encircling the pelvic area was a cracked leather cartridge belt with a holster in which, oddly, a pistol still resided. Convinced that this skeleton was the remains of one of the three men killed by Stockton two years earlier and deducing that it had been washed some significant distance downstream, Upholt directed his search in the opposite direction. While hiking up the arroyo the following afternoon, he found a second skeleton. After examining it closely, he discerned a bullet hole in the skull. One week later and several more yards upstream, the skeleton of the third man was found.

Upholt suggested to Cancino that the men, being lighter, had been carried farther downstream by the flood waters than the horses and mules. He reasoned that continued upstream searches should yield the remains of the animals. If true, this would place them closer to the location where the gold ingots were dumped from the leather panniers.

Another week passed before Upholt found the skeleton

of one of the mules. Nearby he also found a rotted pack saddle and a portion of a pannier. Studying his location, he realized that not far upstream and just over the rim was the sheep herder camp. A few more days passed, and Upholt eventually decided on a site where he was certain he would have an excellent chance at finding the gold. He undertook the excavation of three holes within a wide perimeter he outlined. The work was tedious and exhausting, but Upholt was convinced patience and persistence would eventually lead him to the gold. When he had excavated each hole to a depth of six feet, he employed a probe to try to determine the depth of bedrock, which he found anther nine feet below. The bars of gold, he concluded, would likely have sunk through the fine, loose sands and collected at the level of the sandstone layers beneath. Upholt was becoming encouraged.

Two days later as Upholt widened and deepened the holes he found his first gold bar, approximately seven feet below the surface of the channel. Convinced this was the correct location, he renewed his efforts and discovered two more ingots over the next two days.

When Dolores Cancino arrived at the site a week later, Upholt displayed a total of twelve gold ingots he had found. The next morning the two men rode into Santa Fe, sold the gold, and divided the money. Here, Upholt told Cancino it was necessary for him to travel to Colorado to check on some mining interests he had there and he would return as soon as possible. Then, he suggested, they should hire some laborers to continue with the excavation and recovery of the rest of the gold ingots. After shaking hands with Cancino, Upholt rode away toward the north. He was never seen again, and his disappearance remains a mystery to this day.

Several months later when it was apparent that Upholt was not returning, Cancino decided to resume the excavation himself. On arriving at the arroyo, however, he was discouraged to discover that subsequent flash floods had further modified the channel and refilled the holes.

Not long afterward, Cancino sold his ranch and his sheep herd and moved to Santa Fe where he purchased a small grocery store. He remained there until he passed away thirteen years later. Dolores Cancino never returned to the arroyo to try to relocate the gold.

*   *   *

Cancino Arroyo, as it is still known today, remains remote to most travelers but is occasionally visited from time to time by hopeful treasure hunters who search for the lost ingots they are certain still lie below the sandy bottom. The gold, estimated to be worth well over one million dollars today, has remained elusive yet ever tempting.

THE GOLDEN BELL OF CORRALES

A short distance north of Albuquerque and not far from the banks of the Rio Grande lies the town of Corrales. Long before white settlers arrived here, this general region was part of the homeland of the Tigua Indians who lived on and grew crops of corn, beans, and squash on the rich flood plain for countless generations.

During the early part of the sixteenth century, however, the area was visited by the Spanish explorer Coronado and his soldiers, an event that was to change things forever. Coronado's arrival was soon followed by the eventual domination of the region and subsequent settlement by the Spanish over the next two centuries.

While one of the principal objectives of Coronado and his followers was to locate and mine precious metals, it was the fertile floodplain adjacent to the Rio Grande that attracted many of the subsequent newcomers. Here, crops were planted, livestock grazed, and small towns grew until the Spaniards eventually outnumbered the Indians along the river.

Outside of some early temporary camps and a few missions, one of the first official Spanish settlements in this area was formalized during the early 1700s when the governor of the province provided a land grant to one Franciso

Monte Vigil. A town evolved and was eventually named Corrales. By 1870, the population of Corrales was just under 700 souls, and, as was typical for these kinds of settlements, it was dominated a large Catholic church.

The church, in addition to being a place of worship for the settlers and a growing number of Indian converts, was also a gathering place for a variety of social activities ranging from marriages to celebrations related to the annual harvest. Understandably and justifiably, the residents were quite proud of their church.

As the town of Corrales grew and prospered, the need for a larger church became apparent, and in 1750 a new one was constructed on the west bank of the Rio Grande a few hundred yards north of the present-day Alameda-Corrales bridge. Corrales residents, as well as neighbors from miles around, filled the new building every Sunday for mass.

Around this time, according to legend, a Corrales man was dying from an unknown disease. Physicians could not cure him and he was gradually wasting away. Friends placed him on a litter one Sunday morning and carried him into the church. During the mass, the dying man allegedly rose from his litter, danced among the pews, and pronounced himself cured. The story of the Miracle of Corrales, as the event soon came to be called, quickly spread across the countryside and before long hundreds of people flocked to the church every weekend to attend one or more of the several masses that were now being presented. In a short time, the need for yet another new and larger church had been clearly established.

It was decided by the priest and Corrales residents alike that this new church should have a fine new bell cast in gold. Each week, church members contributed to this cause when the collection plate was passed around—gold coins were tossed in as well as gold rings, earrings, necklaces, bracelets and even nuggets. In time, a significant amount of gold was collected, melted down, and the metal was then cast into a beautiful bell. The new bell was deemed a fine piece of workmanship by all who saw it, and it was so heavy that it reputedly took four men to lift it. One Sunday during the year 1760, the bell was raised to the top of the church where it was installed and rung proudly every subsequent Sunday, holy day, and celebration.

Then, months later, disaster struck.

Following nearly two weeks of heavy rains, the Rio Grande, along with many of its tributaries, swelled to flood stage. A short distance north of town, the waters of the Jemez River, which fed into the Rio Grande, were held back by an earthen dam. During the dry summer seasons, this impounded water was released into a system of canals which carried it to the nearby fields for irrigation. During the rains, the Jemez reservoir overflowed, the water tearing a V-shaped opening in the dam and surging downstream. Lying in the path of these rushing waters was the new Corrales church.

Days later when the flood waters finally receded, residents arrived at the site of the church and gazed in awe at what they found: The structure had been completely washed away.

Resigned to their great loss, the determined Corrales citizens undertook construction of yet another church, this one a substantial, and hopefully safer, distance from the river. All were particularly saddened by the loss of the golden bell which had become a symbol of community pride for the town of Corrales.

*   *   *

Amazingly, the golden bell was found just over a century later and then lost again. The bell was discovered in the bed of the Rio Grande not far from where the old church once stood. It was in December 1865, and as a result of a drought that lasted several months, the water in the river was lower than it had been for years. During this bitterly cold winter, the river often froze over with a layer of ice extending from bank to bank.

Concerned that his cattle were unable to break through the thick ice to reach the shallow water, a rancher sent one of his cowhands to break it open. As the cowhand was chipping away at the ice with an axe, he struck a metal object. Digging away river silt and cobbles, he exposed enough of the object to see that it was shaped like a bell. Though he wasn't certain at the time, he thought it might be made of gold. The cowhand tried to pry the heavy bell from the river sands but was unable to budge it.

Following his supper that night, the cowhand walked over to the main house and told the rancher about his discovery. The rancher, a man named Gonzalez, was familiar with the tale of the lost golden bell of Corrales, and told the cowhand they would return to the site the next morning and try to retrieve it.

It was not to be. Later that night, a severe blizzard struck the area and dropped nearly two feet of snow. The storm forced the rancher and his cowhands to devote their time and energy tending to the livestock. The bad weather continued for almost two weeks. Meanwhile, days of heavy rains several miles upstream caused the Rio Grande to rise dramatically. The location where the cowhand found the bell was now under three feet of water.

It was almost two months later when the river's level had lowered enough such that Gonzalez thought they might be able to find the bell. The cowhand led the rancher, along with several of the town's residents, to the bank of the river where he believed he first encountered the object. After walking several hundred feet upstream and downstream along the bank, the cowhand realized he was unable to remember the exact location. Furthermore, according to some of the residents, the recent flooding by the river caused a number of modifications in the channel.

Since the great weight of the bell precludes its transportation downstream during periods of increased flow, if it is ever found again it will likely be near the site where it was discovered by the cowhand in 1865. It is entirely possible that the bell can be discovered yet again during some reduced flow of the river. It is also quite likely that, with the advanced technology associated with modern-day metal detectors, the chance of locating the golden bell are considerably enhanced.

If discovered, it is estimated this bell would be worth far in excess of one million dollars, with the historical value placed even higher.

BURIED GOLD COINS
IN SAN JUAN COUNTY

During the early 1870s, an oft-used stagecoach route ran between Santa Fe, New Mexico, and Prescott, Arizona. The stage line was owned and operated by the Star Line Nail and Transportation Company and carried mainly people and goods. From time to time, however, SLNT held a contract to deliver military payrolls from time to time.

During the summer of 1874, a SLNT stagecoach was stopped on the road approximately eighty miles east of Santa Fe by two small time outlaws named Tom Horton and Sam Wharton. Two passengers, along with the driver and guard, were robbed of money, watches, and jewelry. The biggest prize, however, was a strongbox filled with just over $50,000 worth of gold coins, all intended as part of a military payroll.

Horton and Wharton cut the horses loose from the coach and drove them off into the nearby hills. Leaving the passengers and employees stranded miles away from any town, the two outlaws then rode away toward the north.

Horton and Wharton had ridden only a short distance when they became acutely aware of the difficulty of transporting the heavy, bulky strongbox. After nearly and hour and with great effort, they finally succeeded in breaking it open. This done, they divided the gold coins and stuffed them into their saddlebags. After a few more miles, however, their already tired mounts were clearly struggling with the significant additional weight of the heavy gold.

After two more miles, Horton and Wharton found themselves riding past an Indian settlement where they spied a number of horses grazing nearby. Realizing their own tired mounts were giving out, they stole three of the ponies. After pulling saddles and bridles from their own horses and placing them on the new ones, they loaded the gold onto the third and rode away. It was believed the two men were attempting to escape into Colorado.

By the time they reached the settlement of Blanco in San Juan County, Horton and Wharton were convinced they had made a clean getaway and that no posse would likely follow them that far. The two men did not figure on the United States Army. Once the report of the stolen payroll reached division headquarters, officers in charge quickly assembled a squad of cavalry and sent them out to capture the two bandits and recover the gold coins.

While Horton and Wharton were purchasing supplies in Blanco, they learned of the cavalry patrol approaching rapidly from the south and not more than three miles away. Quickly riding away in a northwesterly direction, the two outlaws hoped to elude the military pursuit.

The long, hard journey had taken its toll on the three stolen horses the past few days and they were not up to the flight. Wharton decided it would be prudent to hide the gold someplace, deny their involvement in the robbery, and take their chances with the law. When they were finally turned loose for lack of evidence, they were convinced, they would simply return for the gold and continue on to Colorado.

Somewhere between Blanco and Aztec, the outlaws spotted a strangely arch-shaped rock a short distance off the trail. Realizing immediately that it would serve as a recognizable landmark, they excavated a hole in the shadow of the rock and buried the gold coins. This done, they continued on toward Aztec.

Within an hour of caching the payroll, Horton and Wharton were overtaken by the cavalry, placed under arrest, and transported to the nearest army post. Though they were subjected to intense and prolonged questioning, neither of the two outlaws admitted their guilt nor revealed the hiding place of the gold. The two men were eventually tried, convicted, and sentenced to forty years in the state penitentiary.

After serving approximately twelve years of his term, Tom Horton died in prison, a victim of tuberculosis. Wharton was released on parole after serving thirty-five years of his sentence.

Within a year of being released from prison, Sam Wharton returned to northwestern New Mexico to retrieve the gold he had buried over three decades earlier. Living in a rented room in Aztec, he rode out on the trail toward Blanco several days each week searching for the arch-shaped rock that marked the hiding place. For months Wharton searched, but invariably returned to his lonely room empty-handed. One day, Wharton just disappeared. No one saw him leave and he was never spotted in this region again.

*   *   *

In downtown San Francisco in the year 1917 an old man was found dead in his room in a decrepit old hotel. The old building served as a home to derelicts and others down on their luck. Little was known of the old man except that he had lived quietly in the same room for eight years, and that he liked to take short walks in a nearby park and would sit for hours in the warm sunshine on a bench.

He delighted other roomers with stories of working on ranches when he was younger and riding the outlaw trail in New Mexico. He often related a story about himself and a friend who robbed a stagecoach of a military payroll, were pursued by the army, and had to bury over $50,000 worth of gold coins near a curious arch-shaped rock formation somewhere along the trail between Blanco and Aztec. He talked about the long and difficult years in prison. He told of how, when he was released, he returned to the area where he buried the gold and tried to find it but never could.

He died penniless, and his name was Sam Wharton.

SEVENTEEN TONS OF GOLD
BURIED AT FOUR CORNERS

In all the United States, one of the most amazing and baffling tales concerning the relatively recent burial of a massive amount of gold has as its setting a remote portion of desert in the Four Corners area in far northwestern New Mexico in San Juan County where the boundaries of the Land of Enchantment meets those of Colorado, Utah, and Arizona.

During the mid-1930s, approximately seventeen tons of gold were clandestinely flown into this region from Mexico and buried at the top of an isolated mesa. Its retrieval was dependent upon certain economic conditions that never did materialize before the parties involved in caching the fortune had to abandon the site, never to return.

By all accounts, the gold, estimated to be worth more than $16,000,000 at today's values, is still lying concealed in a shallow trench-like excavation near the west end of the bare, eroded mesa near where four states come together.

*   *   *

One June afternoon in 1933, William C. "Wild Bill" Elliot received a strange telegram at the office of the crop dusting service he operated in Midvale, Utah, located just south of Salt Lake City. The message was from a man he didn't know named Don Leon Trabuco, a message which invited him to fly to a small landing strip near Kirtland, New Mexico for a secret meeting. For his effort, Elliot was to be paid $2,500, a rather large sum of money for that time. The message did not say what the meeting was about or how Elliot came to be selected.

Elliot, a native of Salt Lake City, had considerable experience as a pilot. He had worked as a stunt flier for a circus, had owned a charter service, and was working as a crop duster and helping Utah farmers try to eliminate the cricket plague that was devastating much of the state's agricultural productivity at the time. The large fee just to make a 700-mile round trip was appealing, and Elliot quickly agreed to the meeting.

Elliot arrived at the Kirtland landing strip two days later and was climbing out of his Cessna when a tall Mexican in a dark suit approached him and handed him a typed message. The note was from Trabuco and was an invitation for the pilot to meet him at the Kirtland Hotel.

Trabuco was a wealthy landowner, rancher, banker, and businessman living near Puebla, Mexico, a large city located about 100 miles southeast of Mexico City. Years later, Elliot recalled to friends that Trabuco was expensively dressed, very polite, and spoke English extremely well. It was clear he possessed all of the benefits of a formal education and a wealthy lifestyle. It was said, though never substantiated, that Trabuco was descended from the original Spanish conquistadors who conquered Mexico centuries earlier, and that he was the head of a large, prominent, and very powerful family that controlled politics and the flow of money throughout the central part of the country.

An assistant handed Elliot a flight map of an area near Puebla where one of Don Trabuco's large ranches was located. Here, Trabuco told the pilot, he was to pick up a large load of gold ingots. After leaving the ranch, Elliot was to fly an evasive pattern back to the United States, eventually landing at a remote airstrip near a small, isolated mesa located a few miles northwest of Shiprock, New Mexico. Trabuco also informed the pilot of appropriate and safe fuel stops along the way.

Trabuco also told Elliot that this was to be only the first of several trips, and that ultimately a total of seventeen tons of gold was to be delivered at the designated site over a few weeks. For his efforts, Trabuco told Elliot, he was to be paid $40,000 in cash. He also informed Elliot that this, and other business conducted between the two men, was to be kept in the strictest confidence.

Elliot considered the large sum of money and mentally calculated how many planes it would purchase and how he would be able to improve his crop dusting business. With only a few short seconds of deliberation, the pilot readily agreed to the bizarre proposition.

When Elliot asked when he was supposed to pick up the gold, Trabuco told him to be at the Puebla ranch the next day. He then handed Elliot a check for $2,500.

Some time during the late afternoon of the following day, Elliot pulled his plane to a stop at the end of short landing strip adjacent to the Trabuco ranch house. He was immediately met by several guards in uniform, all armed with late model machine guns. While Elliot stood aside and watched, three ranch hands loaded a number of heavy gold ingots into the plane.

The next morning, Elliot took off and flew back to New Mexico. During the 1930s, eluding the border patrol and other law enforcement authorities of both countries was relatively easy, and after many hours he finally landed the gold-laden aircraft on a tiny, rough, and rocky makeshift landing trip adjacent to the specified mesa.

Moments after Elliot cut his engines, a new pick-up truck was driven up to the side of the plane. Out of the truck stepped Don Trabuco himself and two other Mexicans obviously in his employ. Trabuco had exchanged his expensive business suit for a more practical safari jacket, khaki pants, and khaki shirt, and was wearing hiking boots. Elliot noted that several shovels and picks were in the bed of the truck.

The pilot was instructed to stand several yards away as the two workers unloaded the gold from the airplane. As Elliot watched, the Mexicans removed the gold ingots from the Cessna and placed them carefully into the bed of the truck. The gold, according to Trabuco, was to be driven to a location atop the mesa, wrapped and sealed with wax, and buried.

Trabuco told Elliot he would contact him in a few days regarding the next pick up and delivery. The two men shook hands, and as the pilot took off and began his flight back to Midvale, he watched the truck filled with gold laboring up a narrow, twisting dirt road that led up a steep incline toward the top of the mesa.

During the next several weeks, Elliot made a total of sixteen trips to Puebla and back to the Four Corners area. He estimated he had carried a total of 350 gold ingots, each of which he guessed to weigh 100 pounds.

Following the delivery of one of the loads, Elliot became curious as to where the gold was being buried. After taking off and orienting his Cessna in a north-

westerly direction toward his home in Midvale, he cir-
cled around, gradually gaining altitude until he was
soaring at approximately 25,000 feet. As he approached
the mesa, he cut the engines and glided across the
topographic feature in silence. Looking out his window,
he spotted the pick up truck and four men near the
western edge of the mesa. From his high altitude, it
appeared to Elliot the men were excavating a long
trench.

When Elliot made his final delivery, he was invited
to another meeting with Trabuco at the Kirtland Hotel.
There, he was paid the $40,000 promised him. He was
also provided several pages of paperwork that guaran-
teed him a significant bonus in the event that the gold
could be sold at a specified profit in the future.

*   *   *

For the next several years, Elliot watched the rising and falling
prices of gold and noted that the expectations of Don Trabuco were
never met. Elliot regretted this, for he genuinely looked forward to
receiving the promised bonus.

One summer morning, Elliot read in a newspaper that Trabuco
and a number of other prominent Mexican businessmen and
bankers had been charged with corruption and conspiracy to murder and sent to prison. For the next several months, Elliot kept
himself well informed of these developments deep in Mexico from
information fed to him by contacts he had in the area. Then, one
day after coming back from a crop dusting job, Elliot received the
news that Don Trabuco had died in prison.

Elliot was convinced the gold, all seventeen tons of it, still lay
buried in the ground in the long trench he saw being excavated
atop the mesa near Four Corners. He was now determined to
retrieve it for himself.

More time passed, and Elliot's newly formed charter flying
service was growing and making significant profits. As a result, he

found himself unable to break away long enough to try to retrieve the gold.

Presently, World War II broke out and the patriotic Elliot enlisted in the U.S. Army Air Corps. With his flying skills, he was immediately sent to the war theater in England. In December 1944, Elliot was reported missing in action. Two months later, it was discovered that his plane was shot down and he and his co-pilot were killed.

As far as anyone knows, all of the principals associated with the caching of this incredible treasure in gold bars on the mesa near the Four Corners area are now either dead or far, far away in Mexico. According to people who heard Elliot relate his experiences relative to this massive treasure, there is a strong belief among many that it likely still lies atop the mesa, still buried in a shallow excavation.

Because so few people are aware of the existence of this multimillion dollar treasure, only a handful of adventurous souls have ever considered searching for it. As a result, the mesa has rarely been visited.

When Elliot passed away, he left no notes or maps pertaining to the huge fortune in buried gold. He apparently preferred to trust everything to memory. All that is known about this case is what Elliot related to a few of his close friends.

While the mesa in question is not as large as some in this part of the southwestern desert, it still covers hundreds of acres. All that is known from Elliot's conversations is that the treasure is buried somewhere near the west end.

It is still there, still tempting, still luring those who dream of finding this great fortune.

THE LOST DUPONT MINE

For years, Harry Dupont wandered about and explored various mountain ranges throughout New Mexico and Arizona in search of gold and silver. While years passed without Dupont ever making a big strike, he always managed to find just enough ore to sustain him and provide for new prospecting trips. Then one day in 1883, Dupont, along with a young partner, discovered what many have come to believe may be one of the richest gold veins ever found in New Mexico. For a year, Dupont and his partner mined the ore, exchanged it for gold coin, and accumulated a massive fortune.

One day, Dupont was found murdered and his partner presumed dead. The gold mine was never found, and since no one but the two partners knew the location of the mine, it remains lost to this day.

*   *   *

Dupont, in his late forties, was hanging around El Paso, Texas, for a few days looking for part-time work to fund a new grubstake when he met a young man named Frank D. Thompson. Like Dupont, Thompson was a less-than-successful prospector and considerably less experienced. In spite of the fact that Thompson was only twenty years old, the two men got along well and eventually decided to work together as a prospecting team. Almost immediately, they began making plans to return to New Mexico to examine some promising locations. The two men shook hands and agreed that any and all profits were to be shared equally.

Dupont was the more experienced of the two, having been employed in a variety of capacities by several large mining companies over the years. A loquacious sort, Dupont never tired of talking about his knowledge and accomplishments. Thompson, on the other hand, was rather shy and quiet and inclined to let Dupont make the decisions about most matters.

A few days north of El Paso, the two men set up camp and prospected around the Organ Mountains. After three months of finding nothing, they loaded their few posses-sions onto a pair of mules and traveled to Socorro, about 120 miles farther north. Here, they talked to other prospectors and miners and learned about some rich strikes in the Magdalena Mountains, a three-day walk to the southwest. Dupont and Thompson decided to go and try their luck.

In the Magdalenas, Dupont and Thompson had no more success than they had in the Organs, so they abandoned the region after a few weeks and continued on to the little town of Alameda, located just north of Albuquerque. Here they lived in a poor camp just outside of town until they ran out of money.

The year was 1881, and the discovery of copper near the town of Cuba (then called Nacimiento), some sixty miles to the northwest of Alameda, held the promise of jobs. After a long and arduous trek to the region, Dupont and Thompson secured employment that paid them each one dollar per day. The two men decided they would work only long enough to finance another prospecting expedition. For two years they labored in the mines, consistently adding portions of their meager wages to their savings.

When Dupont and Thompson had several days in a row off work, they ranged northward into the Gallina Mountains, always in search of a promising outcrop.

Gallina Peak, the dominant mountain in this Rio Arriba County range, rises to an altitude of 8,977 feet. One day during the summer of 1883, Dupont and Thompson were hiking high along the west side of the mountain just below the timber line when they discovered an outcrop of gold. After having several pieces of it assayed and learning that it was very rich, the partners quit their jobs, moved to the mountain, and established a camp approximately fifty to sixty yards from the vein. Nearby was a small fresh water spring. The forest provided plenty of wood for fuel and wild game was abundant.

Weeks passed, and Dupont and Thompson labored up to fifteen hours per day digging into the mountainside as they followed the vein of gold. As they excavated deeper, they were delighted to note the vein was growing wider and richer. After digging approximately forty feet into the solid granite, they encountered an impressively large pocket of rich, gold-laced quartz. At last, the two men realized, they were going to be very rich.

As the gold-filled chunks of quartz were carried out of the shaft, the rock was crushed and the gold separated and placed into canvas ore pouches. After the two men had filled several pouches with the ore, they decided to carry them into town and exchange the gold for coin. Before leaving, they took great pains to cover the opening to the shaft with brush and pine boughs, making it appear much like the rest of the environment.

Dupont and Thompson traveled to the small settlement of Lagunitas, a few miles south of Cuba, and brought their gold to the Abraham Solomon store. During the time he was employed at the copper mines, Dupont became friends with Solomon and was comfortable conducting business with the merchant.

While Solomon paid coin for the gold, much of the transaction was observed by Isaac and Timothy McCoy, two of the original settlers of Lagunitas. Both men noted that Dupont and Solomon went into the businessman's private office to negotiate the sale of the gold while Thompson was instructed to remain outside. For each week that the two miners claimed they dug their gold, the younger Thompson was paid a twenty dollar gold piece while Dupont pocketed the remainder. When Dupont and Thompson left the Solomon store to return to the mountains, Tim McCoy commented to the merchant that the younger man had just been cheated.

On returning to the camp at Gallina Peak, Dupont carried his share of the gold into the forest and far from the gaze of Thompson. There, he excavated a large hole, lined it with rocks, and placed his share of the gold within. Atop the hole he laid a large, flat rock and covered it over with dirt and debris so that it looked like a part of the forest floor.

Several months passed, and Dupont and Thompson made a number of trips to Lagunitas and the Solomon store to sell their gold. At each visit, Thompson was given a twenty dollar gold piece for each week of labor while Dupont packed the majority of the coins in his saddlebag. At each return to Gallina Peak, Dupont would add his share of the gold coins to his secret cache.

During one visit to Lagunitas, Solomon left the office door slightly ajar while he and Dupont were making the transaction. Thompson happened to pass by and glance in and saw the stacks of gold coins being counted out to his partner. After noting the disparity in the division of profits, he began to realize that Dupont was holding out on him.

On the ride back to Gallina Peak, Thompson asked Dupont about the discrepancy in the division of the gold coins. Dupont became defensive and tried to change the subject, but when Thompson persisted, the older miner claimed that the cost of supplies and equipment came out of the gold in the saddlebags. Thompson reminded Dupont that each man had been purchasing their own supplies from their share of the money. Dupont refused to discuss the matter any further and the rest of the trip was made in angry silence.

Back in Lagunitas, Tim McCoy commented to Abraham Solomon that there was bound to be a falling out between the two miners before long because the older one was clearly robbing the younger one.

During the next several months, more trips were made to Lagunitas to sell the gold. Even though the division was always in favor of Dupont, Thompson never said a word.

In July 1884, the two miners failed to show up at the Solomon store to sell their gold. More weeks passed, and still Dupont and Thompson did not arrive. Out of concern for his friend Dupont, Abraham Solomon organized a search party to ride to Gallina Peak and determine what happened to the two men.

On arriving at the campsite, the members of the search party found the badly decomposed remains of Dupont. His skull had been crushed. Presuming Thompson had also been killed, they searched the immediate area for his body but never found it.

A few days later, the county sheriff conducted an investigation and arrested a sheepherder named Perfecto Padilla for the murder of Dupont and Thompson. The sheepherder admitted observing the two men from a distance as they worked in their mine, but denied killing them. Padilla also admitted to the sheriff that he found Dupont's body weeks earlier and took a watch he found in a pocket.

Padilla was eventually tried, found guilty, and hanged for the murder of Harry Dupont. During the months that followed the execution, Gallina Peak was visited by swarms of prospectors and other hopeful men in search of what was being referred to as The Dupont Mine. The old campsite was located, but so well concealed was the mine shaft that it was never found.

*　　*　　*

In 1892, a man named Manuel Chaves, along with some friends, traveled from their homes near the Colorado border south into the Gallina Mountains to hunt wild turkeys. While scouting alone for turkey sign along the west side of the mountain, Chaves came upon an entrance to a mine shaft that was partially covered with tree limbs and dried brush. Parting the limbs just enough to pass into the old mine, Chavez lit matches and explored a length of the tunnel.

Near the opening, Chaves found a number of rusted mining tools, but what he found at the rear of the shaft took him by surprise: In the dim light of his matches, Chaves encountered a wall of bright, shining quartz laced throughout with seams of gold. In addition, a number of gold-rich quartz rocks were lying scattered about the floor of the shaft. Chaves picked up several and stuffed them into his jacket pockets. He then hurried back to the hunting camp, believing he had discovered a long lost Spanish gold mine. He was determined to keep the information to himself, and for the next few days he made plans to return to the mountain and undertake the extraction of the gold.

Once back home in Colorado, Chaves had the ore assayed and learned that it was extremely rich. He immediately wrote a letter to his father in Albuquerque, telling him of the discovery and including a map to the mine. He asked his father to join him in a few weeks and travel with him to the mine. Unfortunately, the elder Chaves passed away only days later. A search through his belongings failed to locate the map.

More time passed, and Chaves finally found time to return to Gallina Peak. Though he searched for days, he was never able to relocate the mine shaft.

*   *   *

In 1895, a pair of prospectors named Gordon Miller and John Turk were panning for gold and looking for promising outcrops in the Jemez Mountains, about seventy-five miles southeast of Gallina Peak. Here, they learned the story of the Lost Dupont Mine from area sheepherders. Intrigued at the possibility of finding the mine, the two partners decided to travel to the peak to see if they might have any luck searching for it. On reaching Cuba and after acquiring even more information about the mine and the murder of Dupont, they packed their burros and headed for the Gallina Moutains.

Miller and Turk established a campsite near a spring on the western slope near the timberline and set about the business of searching for the mine. At one location, they found a place where gold ore had been separated from quartz, but were unable to find a mine nearby. They also had no luck in locating the campsite of Dupont and Thompson. Since it was late autumn and cold weather and snow was setting in, Miller and Turk decided to abandon the mountains, stay in Alameda for the winter, and return in the spring.

By the time most of the high country snow cover melted off in April, Miller and Turk were back in the Gallina Mountains searching for the mine. One day in late August while exploring along a portion of the western slope just below timberline, the two men discovered a human skull. The skull, like Dupont's, had been crushed, and Miller and Turk assumed the skull belonged to Thompson. At the first opportunity, they reported their find to the Rio Arriba County Sheriff who conducted a brief investigation, concluded the skull must be Thompson's and formally closed the case.

Days later, and not far from where the second skull was discovered, Miller found a large, flat rock that was partially covered by forest debris. Scraping away the pine needles and dirt, Miller lifted the rock and stood in stunned surprise at what he found beneath it. Before him was a stone-lined hole filled with bulging canvas ore sacks. Summoning Turk, the two men removed the sacks, opened them, and were overwhelmed to find hundreds of twenty-dollar gold pieces. They both realized at that moment they had found Dupont's secret cache. Carrying the coins back to camp, they counted them and and found they were $42,600 richer.

Carrying their new-found fortune back to Alameda, Miller and Turk placed it in the bank, keeping out a small amount for living expenses. The two men were convinced that if Dupont had accumulated that much money in the relatively short time he and Thompson dug the gold from the shaft at Gallina Peak, then the mine must indeed be extremely rich. They were determined to return to the mountain the following spring and make another attempt to find it.

Though they worked all through the spring and summer of 1896, the two partners had no success whatsoever at locating the mine. Dejected, they returned to Alameda, withdrew their money from the bank and divided it. Miller took his share and went to Texas to buy a farm. Turk decided to try his luck prospecting in Arizona.

*   *   *

Late one afternoon in 1900, a stranger rode into Alameda on a bay horse and asked where he could find a priest. He was directed to the nearby church, and as he rode toward it he spotted a cleric crossing the road just ahead of him. Riding up to the priest, the stranger handed him a large envelope, turned, and rode away. The priest, believing it was a donation, folded the envelope and placed it in a cassock pocket. Later that evening, he remembered the package, withdrew it, and sat in stunned silence in the glow of a gas lamp as he read it.

It was a confession of murder written by Frank D. Thompson!

The document was several pages long, written by an unskilled hand, was rambling and vague in places, and replete with misspelled words. Essentially, it started out with an expression of remorse that the innocent sheep herder Perfecto Padilla had been executed for a murder he did not commit. In the letter, Thompson admitted to killing Dupont.

Thompson wrote that during his time with Dupont he grew angrier with each passing day about being cheated out of his fair share of the mine's profits. One evening after returning from the Solomon store, Thompson followed Dupont into the woods and watched him hide his coins in the hole and cover it with the flat rock.

Early the next morning, according to Thompson's confession, the two men entered the shaft and resumed their drilling activities. As Dupont, on his knees, held the drill bit steady, Thompson wielded the eight-pound hammer, slamming the bit deeper and deeper into the quartz. As the anger built in Thompson, he was seized with rage and suddenly brought the hammer down onto Dupont's head, killing him instantly. Dropping the hammer, Thompson grabbed his partner's body and dragged it out into the woods. For the next two days, he remained in camp pondering his deed and agonizing over what to do.

Finally, Thompson decided to make Dupont's death appear to be the result of an Indian attack. He returned to the body, scalped it, and cut off one of the ears. He then went to Dupont's cache and removed only as many of the coins as he could stuff into his pockets, leaving the rest. When finished, he recovered the hole with the flat rock.

Taking the two mules, Thompson fled to Albuquerque where he sold them. Here, he lived as a recluse for the next fifteen years. Eventually, his money ran out and, remembering the rich mine on Gallina Peak, he made plans to return to the site and dig for more of the gold.

Weeks later when he arrived in Cuba, he kept to himself for fear of being recognized. During the few days he spent there he learned with regret that the sheepherder Padilla had been hanged for Dupont's murder. He also learned that, as a result of the discovery of the second skull not far from where Dupont's body was found, that he had been declared legally dead.

On arriving at a location on the west side of the mountain where he believed he would find the mine, Thompson encountered a goat pen that had been constructed where the old campsite had been. He talked to the goatherder, but the old man knew nothing about Dupont, the killing, or a gold mine.

For many weeks Thompson searched for the old mine but was unable to find it. During those fifteen years that he was absent from the Gallina range, erosion and overgrazing by the herds of goats on the mountainside had modified the features such that he was unable to recognize any landmarks.

Thompson also spent many hours searching for Dupont's rock-lined cache, hoping to retrieve the rest of the gold coins hidden beneath the flat rock, but could not find it either. Dejected, he returned to Albuquerque and wrote out the long confession.

Weeks passed and Thompson pondered over what to do with the document. Finally, for reasons unknown, he decided to deliver it to the village priest at Alameda. He waited until a week after New Year's day, 1900, and rode horseback to the tiny village.

After handing the envelope to the priest, Thompson rode away, never to be seen or heard from again.

*   *   *

By all accounts, the Lost Dupont Mine is still lost. Judging from how much gold was excavated from the mine by Dupont and Thompson during the time they worked it, it must indeed be a very rich deposit, perhaps, according to experts, potentially one of the richest in all of New Mexico.

NORTHEAST

LOST MILLIONS OF MADAM BARCELO

During the spring of the year 1839, a slow-moving pack train transporting approximately a half-million dollars worth of gold coins was attacked in the foothills of the Sangre de Cristo Mountains in northeastern New Mexico. During the encounter, the coins were hastily buried. Every member of the pack train was killed save for the leader, Raul Cortez, who would die a few weeks later. To this day the location of the buried gold coins, estimated to be worth several million dollars at current values, has never been found.

*   *   *

It was the first week of April 1839 when the noted packer Raul Cortez was summoned to the office of the territorial governor in Santa Fe. Cortez, along with his long time partner Manuel DeGrazi, were well known throughout the Rocky Mountains from Montana to Mexico as competent and trustworthy handlers of freight and goods. As their reputation grew, their services were in great demand among merchants in the rapidly growing settlements of the region. In time, Cortez and DeGrazi came to prefer doing business only with the wealthy, for which they were paid extremely well.

Though enjoying his time of rest in Santa Fe after delivering several wagonloads of goods to merchants, Cortez was quite curious as to why the governor should need his services. After barbering and dressing in his finest attire, he strode to the capital in anticipation of the meeting.

Following a preliminary handshake and a smattering of small talk, Cortez was taken into a well-furnished room and introduced to one Maria Toulos. Known in Santa Fe as Madame Barcelo, Toulos ran the most successful bordellos and gambling houses in all of New Mexico. During the past several years, she explained to Cortez, she had amassed a total of a half-million dollars in profits. Since the young banks in Santa Fe offered little or no security for a fortune that large, she wished to have her gold coins shipped to an established bank in New York City. She explained to Cortez that she would like for him to carry her wealth to the banks of the Missouri River at Independence, Missouri, where it was to be loaded onto a paddlewheel, transported to New Orleans, and thence on to New York via steamer. The coins, she explained further, were to be closely guarded by an armed and mounted contingent of carefully selected fighting men. Madame Barcelo informed Cortez he would be extremely well-paid for his efforts.

Raul Cortez pondered the offer briefly for a moment then eagerly accepted the charge. He did suggest, however, that the pack train would be traveling through a portion of the country filled with hostile Indians and highwaymen, and that a large force of guards would only serve to arouse interest and suspicion. The fewer the riders accompanying the pack train, he maintained, the less significant it would appear to potential bandits. Barcelo agreed to his suggestion.

The following morning, Madame Barcelo's fortune in gold coins was packed carefully into twenty-four specially made leather panniers and attached to wooden pack saddles which were, in turn, strapped to a dozen trail-hardy mules, each one selected by Cortez himself. Cortez preferred mules over horses as pack animals since the heavily laden beasts would be able to handle the steep and often rugged trails that wound over and through the mountains they would soon encounter.

Just before noon, Cortez and DeGrazi, accompanied by only three experienced mule tenders, led the pack train out of Santa Fe and onto the trail that led northeast and into the Sangre de Cristo range.

On the morning of the second day on the trail, one of the mule tenders rode up to Cortez and reported that the pack train was being followed by a band of men. Spurring their mounts to the top of a nearby low ridge, Cortez and the mule tender scanned the horizon and finally spotted a party of ten riders on the trail approximately one mile behind them. After mentioning to the tender that the newcomers would bear watching, the two men then rejoined the pack train.

That evening after camp had been established, the horses and mules staked out to graze, and dinner consumed, Cortez ordered that at least two men were to remain on guard throughout the night, alternating shifts. Two hours later, one of the guards awoke Cortez and told him that the ten riders passed just to the north of the camp and proceeded along the very same trail the pack train was following. The riders, explained the guard, were all Mexican and were well-armed.

The next morning as the packs were being strapped onto the well-rested mules, Cortez warned his men about the possibility of an ambush somewhere along the trail. Cautiously, and visibly tense, the group set out on the trail, each rider carefully scanning the hills and forests for any sign of an attack.

The bandits struck suddenly when the train was approximately forty miles east of the Taos settlement. Out of a nearby arroyo, the ten horsemen surged on horseback, firing pistols into the ranks of the mule tenders. Reacting immediately, Cortez directed his men to the shelter of a jumble of large rocks on the opposite side of the trail. Here, they took up defensive positions. As the mule tenders returned the gunfire, Cortez and DeGrazi herded the animals into a tight circle, leaving the packs on them in the event they would need to effect a hasty escape.

For the remainder of the day, the two opposing forces exchanged sporadic gunfire. The mule tenders were inexperienced marksmen and their shots were often wide of their targets. Just prior to sundown, Cortez made an appraisal of the location in which his party had taken shelter: It consisted of a wide, irregular circle of large weathered granite boulders, the site offering a modicum of protection from men on horseback. Arranged side by side near the center of the circle were three huge granite boulders, each one the size of a two-story house.

Moments after the sun had gone down, the attackers positioned themselves atop some large rocks overlooking the hiding place and searched for positions from which they could fire into the midst of the mule tenders. With no moon, however, the darkness thwarted their efforts. At the first light of dawn the attackers spotted the muleteers and packers milling about their small campfire and commenced firing. DeGrazi was killed immediately, and seconds later one of the mule-tenders fell from a bullet that smashed through his skull.

Cortez and the remaining two muleteers drove the animals under a large boulder with a protective overhang. From this position they were just barely out of the sight of the attackers. Here, Cortez ordered his charges to quickly excavate a grave for their dead companions. Once the single hole was dug, Cortez instructed the men to enlarge it. After placing the two dead men within, Cortez then carefully laid the twenty-four gold-filled panniers atop them and shoveled a covering of dirt over all. Atop this low mound, he built a campfire and set a pot of coffee to boiling.

With the half million dollars well-hidden, Cortez found logic in offering to surrender to the attackers and employing his keen powers of persuasion to convince them they were transporting nothing of value in the hope they would be allowed to continue their journey. Once the bandits departed, reasoned Cortez, he and the two surviving muleteers would simply return for the gold and proceed on toward the Mississippi River.

Cortez tied a white bandanna to the tip of a rifle and summoned one of the muleteers to climb to the top of the closest boulder and wave it as a sign of surrender. Once atop the boulder, the fellow was immediately shot through the chest and fell to the ground. Cortez and remaining muleteer sunk deeper in the protective confines of the hiding place.

Just before sundown, the leader of the bandits called out to Cortez and asked for permission to approach. Cortez agreed, and a tall Mexican, wearing a large sombrero, white peasant shirt and pants and sporting two bandoleros criss-crossed on his chest, walked to within twenty feet of the low campfire. The bandit explained he had knowledge of the shipment of Madame Barcelo's gold coins and that if the treasure were to be turned over to him immediately, Cortez and his companion would be set free and allowed to return to Santa Fe.

As Cortez denied any knowledge of gold coins, several more of the bandits crept up to within a few feet of him and the muleteer, pointed pistols and rifles at their heads, and ordered them to drop their weapons. After throwing down his pistol, the muleteer turned and ran in an attempt to escape. He was immediately shot down in a volley of gunfire from the Mexicans and was dead before hitting the ground.

While two of the bandits guarded Cortez, the others searched the area for the gold-filled panniers. Calmly, Cortez prepared a pot of coffee over the glowing embers of the fire.

Following an hour of searching the immediate area, the bandit leader returned to Cortez and told him to reveal the location of the gold or he would be shot where he stood. Again, Cortez denied any knowledge of gold.

At this point, one of the bandits approached the leader and told him he recognized Cortez as the brother of Father Cortez, a highly regarded priest in a small New Mexico parish located several miles to the south. The bandit argued that Cortez' life should be spared. Instead of killing the packer, the Mexicans tied him to a horse and led him away.

For the next three weeks, the bandits and their prisoner rode south toward Mexico. The leader was now regretting he had not killed Cortez earlier, since he was useless on this journey and was little more than an extra mouth to feed. Even the other bandits grew less and less concerned about Cortez and eventually ignored him altogether. Where before he was bound hand and foot at night, he was now allowed to roam free. The bandits were convinced that Cortez, having no boots, would not be so foolish as to try to escape.

Cortez, however, had other plans. Late one night when all of the bandits were sound asleep, the packer stole one of their horses and rode away back toward the north. Days later, he encountered a road he recognized, one that he knew led to Santa Fe. Two weeks later, a weary, gaunt, bearded, and quite ill Raul Cortez rode into the capital city and sought an audience with his employer, Madame Barcelo.

Weak and dehydrated, Cortez was carried to a room in Madame Barcelo's gambling establishment and placed on a bed. A physician was summoned, and while he was examining Cortez, the packer explained to Madame Barcelo that her gold was safely hidden in the mountains about forty miles east of Taos. With shaky hand, Cortez sketched a rough map showing the approximate location of the gold cache. He told Madame Barcelo that as soon as he recovered, he would organize an expedition to the site, retrieve the gold, and proceed with it to Independence and the Missouri River. Following that, he lay back onto the bed and fell into a deep slumber.

Raul Cortez never awoke from his sleep. The following afternoon was pronounced dead by the physician.

Two weeks later, Madame Barcelo, along with three investors, organized a party of men to travel to the area described by the dying Cortez and retrieve the gold. Madame Barcelo entrusted the map to the leader of the expedition. Another two weeks passed and no word was heard from the party. With the help of the Santa Fe mayor, yet another expedition was organized. Two days later, the remains of the members of the first group were found along the trail approximately twenty-five miles northeast of Santa Fe, all dead and scalped. The map drawn by Cortez containing the only known directions to the huge gold cache was missing.

*   *   *

Researchers familiar with the tale of Madame Barcelo's treasure of gold coins are convinced the fortune still lies buried somewhere among the jumble of rocks in the foothills of the Sangre de Cristo Mountains where Cortez and his muleteers took refuge against the attack from the

Mexican bandits. The gold, estimated to be worth well over two million dollars today, continues to lure treasure hunters to the region.

LOST SPANISH GOLD MINES IN THE SANDIA MOUNTAINS

Lying just to the north and slightly east of Albuquerque are the Sandia Mountains, granite intrusions formed deep below ground eons ago when molten, pressurized magma was forced from deep within the earth surfaceward through faults and fissures. Never able to break through to the surface, the magma cooled slowly thousands of feet below, eventually solidifying into a hard, durable granite. During the cooling process, gold was formed in a number of places in the thick, dense mass of rock.

More time passed—millions of years—and the several square mile huge granite mass was slowly yet inexorably uplifted and pushed toward the surface as a result of a variety of processes involving pressure and folding in the earth's crust. At the same time, the erosive action of water and wind removed topsoil and overlaying rock and exposing more of the granite. In time, this huge mass rose several hundred feet above the ground, reaching toward the sky. In a number of locations along the flanks of this young mountain range, some of the seams of gold were exposed to the elements, and, eventually, to the inquisitive eyes of men who came looking for it.

*   *   *

The foothills and neighboring environs of the Sandia Mountains have long been home to man. Abundant evidence exists to substantiate the notion that Paleo-Indians hunted game here, raised crops of corn and squash, and generally lived peacefully along the eastern margins, somewhat protected from the bitterly cold west winds by the range. During the sixteenth, seventeenth, and eighteenth centuries, various tribes of American Indians took up habitation in the area. Some were transient, remaining only long enough to hunt game or wait out inclement weather or cold winters. Others stayed for long periods of time, sometimes many generations. These more sedentary Indians tended extensive fields of corn and other vegetables and lived in established villages.

Those who resided the longest in the shadows of the Sandias were the Pueblo Indians, the dominant tribe in the region when the Spanish Explorers arrived during the late 1500s.

The Spanish came to explore, to conquer, and to convert. It is also well known that the conquistadores had orders to search for precious minerals such as gold and silver and, when found, establish and operate mines to harvest the ore which was to be processed and shipped back to the motherland Spain.

It is a matter of historical record that the Spanish did, in fact, find gold and silver in great quantities throughout much of the American West, with New Mexico being particularly rich. Among the extensive deposits of gold mined here by the Spaniards were several locations in the Sandia Mountains, locations which, according to documents, yielded millions of dollars worth of ore, locations that were still rich with gold at the time they were abandoned, locations which were once carefully hidden and are still searched for today.

*   *   *

The Spanish explorers gave the mountain range its name—the Sandias. The word means "watermelons," and it is believed that it was inspired by the reddish color that is prominent along the west side as the setting sun illuminates the mineral rich, red-tinted granite.

The Spanish were quick and efficient in establishing working mines once the gold was discovered. By 1680, at least five mines were in operation in the Sandia Mountains, each of them highly productive. The mines were named The Montezuma, The Window Mine, The Ladder Mine, The Nepusemo Mine, and the Coloa Mine. Existing documents suggest the Montezuma Mine was the richest. Around 1687, according to documents, the Montezuma yielded twelve mule loads of large ingots of almost pure gold, all of which were transported to Mexico City via mule train.

As the productivity of the mines grew, and as shafts were extended deeper and deeper into the mountainside, the need for more workers grew. Before long, the Spaniards were enlisting the help of local Pueblo Indians. Some of these Indians worked in the mines for a short time, but the Pueblos were generally disinclined toward such labor, preferring instead to pursue hunting and fishing in the open air. Eventually, most of them quit the mines.

In response, the Spaniards, with the encouragement of and cooperation from the church, began to actively enslave the Indians, chaining them together, and forcing them to work long hours in the mines for no pay and very meager rations. Platoons of armed Spanish soldiers rode up and down the Rio Grande Valley visiting dozens of Pueblo Indian villages and capturing healthy young men to work in the mines. Many of the slaves died from overwork, starvation, and cave-ins. Some who refused to work were simply killed. It has long been said that whoever locates and enters these mines will find the skeletons of dozens, if not hundreds, of those poor souls who gave their lives so that Spain and the church could grow richer.

Working in the Sandia Mountain gold mines was often dangerous. At least two of the mines were so deep that it was difficult to keep water levels down where some of the richest veins were being worked. Reports of Indian miners drowning in flooded shafts are numerous.

Because most of the mines were vertical, ladders were used as transportation from the surface down to the locations of the veins. The ladders were little more than notched logs (called chicken ladders), and the Indians, bearing leather bags of ore or water or talus climbed up and down these precarious structures, many of them falling to their deaths.

Outside each mine was an arrastre for crushing the gold-bearing rock in order to remove the ore, as well as a forge for melting the gold prior to pouring it into ingots. To this day, one can still find the old arrastres and slag piles where the gold was worked by the Spaniards. Somewhere not far from these arrastres and slag piles, one must assume, are the openings of the mines that still contain a king's fortune in gold.

In August 1680, the Pueblo Indians decided they had endured more than enough slavery and domination at the hands of the Spanish. They organized and initiated a massive and violent revolt to rid themselves once and for all of the Spanish rule that had long since destroyed the peace and tranquility of their homelands. Following the first few raids on Spanish outposts, warnings spread up and down the Rio Grande Valley as well as a number of outlying areas. In response to this threat, the Spaniards fled southward into Mexico for safety. Before leaving, however, they were ordered by the government and the church leaders to close all of the mines and cover them so that no one would ever be able to find them. The Spanish reasoned that when the revolt was finally quelled, they would return to the area, reopen the mines, and continue extracting the gold.

The five gold mines in the Sandia Mountains were effectively filled in and covered over and the camps and settlements in the area quickly abandoned. During the following decade, continued erosion and the new growth of trees and brush caused the reclaimed locations to appear much like the rest of the mountainside.

Before the Pueblo revolt ran its course, it was estimated that at least 400 Spaniards, including two dozen priests, were slain. What mines were not completely closed down and entirely covered up by the Spaniards were sealed off by the Pueblos. The Indians were determined that members of their tribe would no longer be enslaved and forced to labor for the hated Spaniards in the gold mines.

*   *   *

Before the year 1692 was finished, the Spanish had returned to the area of the Sandia Mountains and once again went about the business of conquest and domination. Vastly outnumbered and outarmed, the Pueblos once again fell to Spanish rule, and plans were immediately formulated to resume mining the rich gold in the range.

When the Spaniards set about trying to reopen the mines, they encountered great difficulty in locating the carefully concealed entrances. They enlisted the help of Pueblo Indians who had worked in the shafts twelve years earlier, but the Indians refused to provide any information even though they were subjected to brutal whippings and other forms of torture. In time, two of the mines were finally relocated by the Spanish and reopened, and production was begun anew. The three remaining mines were never found.

Eventually, as a result of the ongoing and sometimes incomprehensible global politics of the time, significant decisions were made by leaders in far away places, and the Spanish, as rulers, were eventually forced to abandon New Mexico and much of the rest of the American West. Once they were gone, the Pueblos again went about the task of reclosing the mines and concealing the entrances such that no one would ever find them again.

It is believed by many, and with good evidence, that even today there are a number of Pueblo elders who allegedly know the locations of the old gold mines, but tribal custom and law does not allow them to reveal the secrets.

*   *   *

Dick Wooten, the famous mountain man and friend of Kit Carson, learned about the lost Spanish gold mines in the Sandia Mountains while living in the region and was determined to find them. Alone, he searched for weeks throughout the range but with no success.

One day, Wooten met and befriended an old Pueblo Indian and asked him if he knew anything about the old mines. The Indian said he, as well as several other members of the tribe, knew the exact locations of the mines but were forbidden to tell anyone. Wooten pleaded with the old man, offered him money and gifts, but to no avail. Finally, after several days of badgering from Wooten, the Indian said he could not tell the white man about the locations of the mines, but if Wooten were to follow him into the Sandia Mountains and observe various places he would stop, he would likely be able to determine the locations for himself.

As Wooten trailed the old Pueblo throughout portions of the Sandia range, he encountered numerous Spanish signs scratched into exposed rock and on the trunks of trees. One such set of signs directed Wooten to a location that appeared slightly different from the rest of the mountainside. After digging into a few feet of rock and debris, Wooten uncovered the entrance to a very old mine shaft. Weeks of heavy labor was sufficient to remove several more tons of rock, eventually exposing approximately eight feet of the old shaft. Having a number of businesses to which he needed to devote his time, Wooten was never able to complete the work of reopening the old Spanish mine. Today, this location is still known by many as "The Old Wooten Mine."

During the late 1800s, stories of the lost Spanish gold mines in the Sandia Mountains circulated throughout much of New Mexico and the rest of the American Southwest. Prospectors and treasure hunters climbed and explored about the range in great numbers for the next few years, but none of the old shafts were ever located.

*   *   *

Not all of the gold discovered in the Sandia Mountains is in the range. Apparently, during the transportation of the gold ingots out of the Sandia Mountains and thence on the long journey to Mexico, some of the gold was dropped and lost.

During the early part of the twentieth century, a farmer named Feliz Zamora was plowing his field when his blade kicked up a fifteen-inch-long gold bar of the purest quality. Zamora sold it for almost $2,000. Not long afterward, a neighbor found a similar gold ingot, this one selling for $1,500. In 1972, yet another gold bar, this one bearing church symbols on one side, was found in an agricultural field not far from the Rio Grande. This discovery prompted a protracted search for more of the bars, two of which were eventually found. The likelihood that more lie just below the surface of these rich farmlands is great.

*   *   *

The search for the lost Spanish gold mines of the Sandia Mountains continues today. Existing documents indicate that when the Spaniards abandoned the range they left untold millions of dollars worth of gold in the mines that were covered over and hidden. To date, no significant evidence exists than any of these mines has ever been effectively reentered, leaving us to consider that the gold is still there.

SANGRE DE CRISTO TREASURE

N ot far to the north of Taos and just a short distance east of the present-day town of Arroyo Seco lies a stream called Arroyo Hondo. This drainage channel flows out of the adjacent Sangre de Cristo Mountains, the waters tumbling over the rocky bottom on their way to lower elevations. To this day, weekend prospectors come to Arroyo Hondo to pan for the tiny gold nuggets that can still be found at the bottom of the stream, sometimes in very impressive quantities.

The amounts of gold taken from Arroyo Hondo these days, however, are a mere fraction of the immense treasure of that precious metal that is hidden somewhere in a shaft somewhere not very far away in the neighboring Sangre de Cristo Mountains.

*   *   *

One cool autumn day in 1671, a young monk from a nearby settlement was walking along the banks of Arroyo Hondo gathering firewood. Just as he had accumulated an armload and was about to turn back toward the small village a short distance away, his eyes caught the glitter of something bright and shiny in the stream bed. Dropping his load of wood, the monk investigated and was surprised to discover a rich deposit of placer gold in the shallow waters. The monk managed to gather a few of the tiny flakes of gold and placed them in a pouch inside his cassock.

Each time the monk was sent out to procure firewood, he would stop by the arroyo and harvest a few more pieces of the placer gold. He observed that as he explored farther upstream, the amount of gold increased, and he intuited, correctly, that if he continued on he would eventually locate the source which, he assumed was very rich.

During one trip to the arroyo, the monk discovered that beyond a certain point in the stream the gold disappeared altogether. Retracing his steps, he returned to the location where the concentration was the greatest. Here, he could find no exposed vein of gold in or near the stream, but he did find traces tiny flakes and nuggets on the slope. The monk realized that the source of the gold was higher up the slope, likely an exposed vein from which these small pieces were being weathered and carried by gravity downslope and thus into the stream. Months passed, and at every opportunity the monk continued his search for the source of the gold.

Then one day he found it. Just as he suspected, he discovered a vein of gold-laced quartz lying exposed to the elements higher up on the slope. The thickness of the vein and the density of the gold within suggested to the monk that this must indeed be an incredibly rich deposit.

Now, the monk decided, was the time to inform his superiors at the Taos mission of his discovery.

One evening about a week following the discovery of the vein, the monk requested an audience with the two priests who were given charge of the mission. After pouring out a quantity of gold onto the table, the monk told of how he discovered it, of his search for the mother lode, and how he found it on a west-facing slope in the Sangre de Cristo Mountains.

Eyeing the gold covetously, Father Antonio de Mora asked pertinent questions about the location and quantity of the rich ore. Then he asked the young monk who else knew of its existence. When the monk told him no one, de Mora cautioned him to keep the information between the three men in the room. He explained that if the church officials learned of the gold they would send soldiers and miners to take it away to Mexico City. The gold, whispered de Mora, could be put to better use among ourselves.

As the three men quit the room and repaired to their respective chambers, Father de Mora pondered the possibilities of the great wealth that lay just a few miles away in the mountains. He began making plans pertinent to mining the gold, having it cast into ingots, and becoming wealthy. As he fell asleep that evening, Father de Mora caressed a piece of the gold-laced quartz he carried to bed with him.

During the next few weeks, de Mora went about the task of collecting laborers to work in the new mine. From the jail cells of garrisons associated with the nearby missions he was provided a number of captive Pueblo Indians. From the fields he enlisted the services of others until he had a total of some seventy men to dig for the gold. They were immediately put to work excavating the ore as well as building an arrasatre and a forge. A supply of wood needed to be cut and hauled to the site to keep the forge burning, so de Mora employed wood gatherers. Food in the form of wild game had to be procured, so de Mora hired professional hunters. It was an intensive operation, but one that yielded great quantities of rich gold ore almost at the outset.

For ten years the mining proceeded, all under a heavy cloak of secrecy. The last thing de Mora wanted was for church officials to learn about and confiscate his great and growing fortune.

In time, the men who worked in the mines became little more than slaves. They were no longer paid for their labors. When a number of them threatened to quit, they were shackled and chained. Furthermore, the miners were forced to work longer days on reduced rations and were often whipped when production lagged. Sadly, many died in the mines from malnutrition and overwork.

As the golden ingots were collected, they were carried to the mission and stored in a spare room. Every evening, Father de Mora would enter the room to count and recount the bars. As he pondered the gold, he dreamed of what this great fortune would bring him.

As the workers died or became too infirm to continue, de Mora found himself constantly in need of more slaves. Using the help of soldiers he bribed, the priest managed to acquire additional workers from the neighboring Indian tribes, all young, healthy men who were taken by force and slapped into chains.

As time passed and the work progressed, the shaft penetrated deeper and deeper into the mountainside and more gold was accumulated. Father de Mora was, indeed, growing wealthy. According to documents maintained by de Mora, documents that were found years later, the Sangre de Cristo mine, during its ten years of operation, yielded an estimated ten million dollars worth of ore in seventeenth century values. According to researchers, this could possibly have been one of the richest gold mines in the world.

During the latter part of the 1670s, the Pueblo Indians, who resided throughout much of this region of New Mexico, were growing weary of the Spanish domination. When the Spaniards arrived, they began overhunting the game, trespassing on heretofore Indian lands, and, worst of all, were prone to enslaving young Pueblo men and women and forcing them to work in less-than-desirable conditions. The inevitable eventually happened: The Indians revolted and were soon waging open warfare on all the Spaniards they encountered. Enslaved Indians were freed, and Spaniards were slaughtered for miles up and down the Rio Grande river valley.

As the hostilities between the Pueblos and the Spanish increased, the church ordered the evacuation of all of its priests and converts from the area and an immediate return to Mexico City. Before abandoning the Sangre de Cristo mine, Father de Mora, with the aid of several monks, loaded the gold ingots onto burros and transported them the twenty miles from the mission to the mine where they stacked them like cordwood along one wall of the extensive shaft. The opening of the mine was then covered with rock and debris and any evidence of tailings was eliminated.

Returning to the church, de Mora wrote a report detailing the existence of the mine and its general location, the activities associated with extracting the gold, and the ultimate accumulation of hundreds of ingots. When finished, the priest hid the manuscript beneath the altar and made plans to leave for Mexico City the following day. Within the week, a war party of Pueblo Indians arrived at the mission and slaughtered all who remained.

For twelve years the Spanish were absent from the region and life began returning to normal for the Pueblos. Then, in 1892, General Don Diego de Vargas arrived in the region with a large contingent of foot soldiers and cavalry. The general waged war on every Indian tribe he encountered, none of whom were any match for the well armed and well trained military. By the time de Vargas was finished, all of the Indians along the Rio Grande Valley had been subdued.

Before long, priests, settlers, and more soldiers arrived
from Mexico City and began to move back into the region
and reclaim what was once theirs. As the new arrivals dug
through the remains of Father de Mora's church, they discovered the manuscript describing the rich gold mine lying
just to the north. Plans were immediately formulated to
locate and reopen the mine.

Now that the secret of the mine was out, however, a
number of expeditions unendorsed by the church set out
for the Arroyo Hondo area to search for it. While de Vargas
and his forces were conquering the Pueblos, dozens of
Indians managed to escape the vengeful wrath of the
Spaniards and were living in the Sangre de Cristo
Mountains. When the gold seekers arrived, they were
immediately attacked and killed. Father Carbonel, the
new priest formally assigned to head the mission, sent five
monks and two dozen soldiers into the Arroyo Hondo area
with directions to the gold mine, but all were killed,
scalped, and mutilated by the Indians.

For over a century, few dared enter the Sangre de
Cristos in search of the lost gold mine because of the
threat of Pueblos. By the mid-1830s, however, most of the
Indians were gone from the mountains. Knowing this, and
having often heard the legend of the lost Arroyo Hondo
gold, one Simon Turley entered the region and began
searching for the mine. Turley found a substantial amount
of placer gold in Arroyo Hondo creek—enough, in fact, to
make him wealthy—but he could never locate the mine.

Father de Mora was never able to return to the Arroyo
Hondo area to reclaim any of the vast fortune he was
forced to leave. So great was the priest's passion for secrecy and for hiding the rich gold mine of the Sangre de
Cristos that it, along with the incredible treasure stored
within it, remains hidden today. It is estimated that
stacked deep within the main shaft of this mine are thou-

sands of ingots of gold bars, all covered with a fine layer of dust as a result of lying undisturbed for over three centuries.

Raton Pass Treasure

William Wooten was often described as a hermit, a recluse, for he preferred to live alone just off the trail that wound high and twisting through the 7,800 feet altitude in Raton Pass in Colfax County, just a few miles from the Colorado border. Some even regarded the old man as crazy but it is more likely that he just liked living by himself and was uncomfortable around others. Wooten seldom traveled to the tiny settlement of Raton located just to the south of the pass, and when he did he generally eschewed the company of all, preferring instead the solitude of his high altitude habitation.

Wooten also had a reputation for being a miser, and by all accounts his miserly ways eventually generated an accumulation of gold and silver coins that, according to those who knew him, filled several used powder kegs. When Wooten passed away, the secret locations of his buried, coin-filled kegs went with him, kegs that, for the most part, are buried today somewhere on Raton Pass awaiting discovery by some lucky, skilled and patient hunter of lost treasures.

*　　*　　*

No one was ever certain where William Wooten came

from and an examination of the history sheds little or no light on the matter. When Wooten arrived in the little settlement of Raton, New Mexico, in 1870, he was regarded as odd and eccentric and generally avoided by the townsfolk. Wearing several layers of old, filthy, ragged clothes and sporting an unkempt head of hair and a woolly beard, Wooten lived in a ragged camp on the outskirts of town and ventured into the business district only rarely to purchase a few supplies. He always paid with coins he pulled out of a small, dirty, leather pouch he kept in a coat pocket.

During the spring of 1871, Wooten loaded his few pitiful belongings onto a swaybacked mule, abandoned his camp, and traveled to a location high up on Raton Pass where the trail was squeezed between the high granite walls of the mountain through a narrow valley. Here, the old man constructed a crude cabin of log and rock, stuffing the chinks with dried juniper foliage. As soon as his cabin was livable, Wooten began working on improving the trail by removing rocks and boulders, blasting away portions of the mountain here and there to make it wider, and generally smoothing it out. This accomplished, Wooten settled in and began charging a toll from all of the travelers and freight wagons that passed.

Wooten seldom strayed far from his cabin for the next eight years, riding into town on rare occasions to purchase a bit of food and some blasting powder. Following each purchase, he loaded his goods onto his mule and hurried back to the pass to collect tolls.

Traffic through Raton Pass generally increased and grew relatively heavy during the 1870s. Travelers and freight wagons made the trip from Santa Fe, Taos, Las Vegas and other points in the south to destinations that lay to the north in Colorado and elsewhere. For the eight years that he operated the toll road, Wooten collected enough coins to fill a number of used powder kegs.

During one visit to town, Wooten remained long enough to visit with another old-timer, a man named Buchanan. Buchanan was a drifter, a sometime prospector who seldom had any luck, and who earned a meager living by sweeping out the bars during the early morning hours and whitewashing barns, stores, and other structures.

For reasons unknown, Wooten informed Buchanan of his hoard of coins and told him they were buried in different locations, all just a short distance from the cabin. When Buchanan asked Wooten what he was going to do with his fortune, the old miser just smiled and said he liked to dig it up once in a while just to look at it and count it.

As Wooten grew older he became increasingly absent-minded. One afternoon while he was in Raton purchasing supplies, he confessed to Buchanan that he had forgotten where he had buried some of his coin-filled kegs. When Buchanan offered to help him find them, Wooten refused and told him no one was ever invited to come to the cabin.

William Wooten passed away in 1878 without ever revealing the locations of his buried kegs. Only days after he was buried, dozens of men, among them Buchanan, swarmed into the pass to try to find the cached treasure. Though they searched for weeks, none were ever located.

Another old-timer who lived in and around Raton was an elderly gent named Cicero Lackey. Lackey eventually took up residence in Wooten's old cabin and told everyone who asked that he was searching for the buried coins. Approximately eighteen months after relocating at Raton Pass, Lackey found one of the kegs. He carried several handsfull of Wooten's coins into town and treated anyone and everyone to drinks at a bar. When asked, Lackey stated he found the keg within only twenty feet of the old cabin.

Lackey remained in the Wooten cabin for several more weeks and continued to search for the remaining kegs, but he never found any. According to relatives, he gathered up the coins he did find and moved to Arizona.

                    *   *   *

In 1972, a man named Tolliver parked his car just off the paved highway that winds through Raton Pass today. Accompanied by his young son, Tolliver spent the afternoon exploring along portions of the old trail not impacted by the newer blacktop. From pervious research, Tolliver learned that in addition to Wooten's cabin, there were a number of semi-permanent campsites along the trail throughout the pass, and he thought he might get lucky and find some interesting artifacts from those bygone days. Though he had read an account about toll master Wooten, Tolliver was, at the time, unaware of the amazing tale of his buried caches of coins.

After two hours of hiking and exploring, Tolliver and his son had accumulated a number of old bottles, some bent and rusted flatware, and even a pair of eyeglass frames that were estimated to be at least one hundred years old.

At one point while searching around the ruins of Wooten's old cabin, Tolliver's son showed his father some pieces of rotted wood that could only have been staves from a small keg, one that would likely have held powder or nails. He explained he found the pieces of a collapsed keg exposed from a hole in the ground several yards away where runoff from rains had eroded away part of the surface. Deeming the wooden staves to be of no import whatsoever, Tolliver encouraged his son to discard them and the two continued with their search.

Several months later, Tolliver heard the story of

Wooten's buried coins stuffed into wooden powder kegs and buried near the old cabin. He immediately recalled his son's discovery of the staves during their previous trip to the region and began making plans to return.

Within three weeks, Tolliver and his son arrived at the pass and undertook to retrace their steps from the previous visit. Though they searched all day long, they were unable to locate the site where the wooden staves were found. Tolliver returned to the pass at least one dozen times to look for the treasure, but each time came away unsuccessful.

*   *   *

Researchers generally agree that the tale of Wooten's buried coins is authentic and are convinced the majority of the kegs still lie hidden somewhere in the pass near the old cabin and are yet to be found. It is difficult to estimate the value of Wooten's buried coins—some say tens of thousands of dollars. Others insist it would be in the neighborhood of hundreds of thousands of dollars.

Regardless of the value, the treasure is, as far as anyone knows, still lying in the ground somewhere near the ruins of the old Wooten cabin in Raton Pass.

SAINT AUGUSTIN MISSION TREASURE

Between the towns of Santa Rosa and Las Vegas, New Mexico, and along the banks of the Gallinas River, a tributary to the Pecos River, lie the ruins of an old Spanish settlement, one that dates back to the early 1700s. Dominating the little village of San Augustin was the Catholic mission, and the priest, along with the village alcalde, oversaw the community of mostly Indian converts to Christianity.

The padres who first arrived at the site believed it ideal for the establishment of a mission: There was plenty of fresh water from the river, an abundance of timber, and the nearby mountains and forest teemed with wild game. Unknown to them at the time, however, was this this location was along an oft-used trail traveled by raiding Apache Indians.

Within only a few paces from the ruins of the old San Augustin mission and just a few inches below the surface lies buried twenty ingots of gold and twenty ingots of silver. These items have been cached at this secret location for over two centuries and if ever found would provide an incredible fortune to the one who chanced upon them.

*   *   *

During the settlement of San Augustin, hostile Apaches were actively raiding throughout the region. Travelers, miners, and settlers were frequent targets of the Indians who sought to remove the trespassers. Though often warned that the location selected for the settlement of San Augustin was nearly indefensible from an attack, the church officials proceeded with the plans to establish a community, all the while maintaining that God would protect them from the heathens.

Among the citizens of San Augustin were a few Mexicans who were engaged in mining gold and silver from the nearby mountains to the west. After the ore was removed from a shaft, it was melted down in a crudely made furnace and poured into molds fashioned from portions of thick stalks of cane that grew in profusion along the banks of the Gallinas River.

From the miners, the church exacted a quinta, the royal fifth that was a form of tax and which would ultimately be forwarded to church headquarters in Mexico City. The miners willingly paid their quinta in the form of gold and silver ingots which they carried to the mission regularly.

As time passed, a total of forty ingots accumulated at the mission—twenty of gold and twenty of silver. The ingots were stored in the priest's quarters until such time as a more suitable location could be found.

For several weeks, San Augustin residents reported seeing mounted and armed Indians watching the town from across the river. Suspecting that the Indians were planning a raid, the citizens began making preparations. The mission priest, convinced the Apaches would seize the gold and silver, carried the ingots several paces from the mission and buried them in a shallow hole. After hurrying back to the church, he drew a crude map showing the location of the ingots, tore it in half, and gave one of the portions to the alcalde, the chief administrative officer. Both pieces of the parchment were necessary for locating the cache of ingots.

Three days later, as expected, San Augustin was attacked by the Indians. A large percentage of the citizens were killed during the raid, among them the alcalde. The priest fled to Mexico, never to return.

Weeks later, visitors to the devastated settlement described San Augustin as being in ruins, the burned-out mission and surrounding houses little more than rubble. Months later, the few survivors of the community resolved to rebuild the town but at a more suitable location. A new site was selected some eight miles upstream on the Gallinas River where it can be found today.

A number of the San Augustin citizens who knew of the gold and silver ingots that were stored in the mission searched the ruins of the church but never found them. The priest was the only survivor of the massacre who knew the location of the treasure cache and he was never seen again and what became of him was never learned.

* * *

During the 1950s, it was learned that a physician living in nearby Las Vegas had in his possession one half of the parchment map drawn by the priest. Using the map, he and one of his sons tried on several occasions to find the cache of ore but were never successful.

A few years later, another man arrived at the old San Augustin settlement, set up a crude camp, and spent many hours searching among the ruins. When local residents inquired about his activities, the newcomer told them that he lived in Colorado and possessed one-half of a very old map that purported to show the location of gold and silver ingots buried near the ruins of the old mission.

The Coloradan was told that the other half of the map was in the possession of the physician who lived only a few miles away. Several days later, the two men spoke on the telephone, but were unable to arrive at any agreement relative to the search for and ultimate division of the buried ingots. Each demanded a lion's share of the recovered treasure. Disappointed, the newcomer returned to Colorado and never returned.

To this day, the San Augustin treasure still lies buried at some unknown location close to the ruins of the old mission.

SECRET PUEBLO GOLD MINE

For the most part, the vast majority of North American Indian tribes had little use for precious metals such as gold and silver, and the notions held by the early settlers relative to value, currency, and holding property were alien concepts to the natives who occupied this new world.

Regardless of their philosophies concerning wealth, many Indians did, however, mine gold and silver in small quantities for use in fashioning ornaments such as arm and wrist bands, earrings, and necklaces. With the arrival of the white man, the Indians soon learned to barter gold and silver for guns and ammunition. Known to many North American Indians were secret locations of outcrops of gold and silver, a number of which, when encountered by early prospectors and miners, eventually became significant producers of ore.

One such mine, one that produced impressive quantities of gold, was used by the Indians who resided near the Cerro de Lauriana, a range located a short distance west of the Gallinas River valley near Las Vegas in San Miguel County. Small amounts of gold were taken from the mine from time to time, and it is believed by most researchers that the rich vein of ore that supplied them has barely been tapped.

*   *   *

During the Pueblo Indian uprising during 1680, Spanish settlers and missionaries living in scattered parts of New Mexico were either killed or driven away. Much of the raiding took place up and down the Rio Grande valley, but outlying Spanish settlements miles away were also attacked and sacked. One such settlement was San Augustin located near the banks of the Gallinas River. Years after the raid, San Augustin was moved to a more defensible location several miles upstream and gradually resettled over the next two decades. Save for subsequent sporadic Indian attacks, San Augustin was a growing and prospering community. One such attack occurred during the first decade of the eighteenth century. During the raid, a young boy named Jose Lucero was taken captive.

Lucero remained with the Indian tribe for the next four years. His life was very difficult, for he was little more than a slave and was put to work gathering firewood and hauling water. He was beaten often by the men of the tribe, the women were inclined to subject him to humiliation and torture, and he existed on scant rations while sleeping out in the open all year long.

During his time as a captive, Lucero occasionally witnessed small parties of Indians riding into camp with saddle pouches bulging with gold nuggets. He watched with interest as the gold, apparently very rich and pure, was hammered out into a variety of ornaments used to adorn men, women, and children alike. From what he could understand of the conversations he overheard, Lucero discovered that the gold came from a small mine located high up in the nearby mountains.

The entrance to the mine was little more than a tiny hole one had to wriggle through with some effort, and it was in a place where it could not be seen unless one was standing directly in front of it. Approximately fifty yards from the mine, Lucero discovered, was a small spring around which grew a stand of low-growing trees. Given the large nuggets and the high quality of the ore, Lucero thought this must indeed be a very rich mine.

Unable to endure his pathetic life as a slave much longer, Jose Lucero began making plans to escape. He made his move late one evening when he believed the time was right. Several of the men had gone to mine some of the gold, a trip that often lasted three or four days, and the rest rode south to hunt for wild game. Lucero was left in camp with women and old men, most of whom had begun to generally ignore him.

So accustomed had the members of the tribe grown to Lucero that they no longer tied him up at night. Instead, he was permitted to wander freely through the camp, with the Indians secure in the belief that he was too frightened to flee.

When he was certain everyone was asleep, Lucero slipped away from the village and began picking his way slowly along a trail in the dark toward his far away home of San Augustin. It was several days later when a haggard and gaunt Jose Lucero staggered into the village. He was reunited with his family and gradually nursed back to health.

After he had recovered, Lucero regaled San Augustin residents with stories of his life as a captive among the Indians. He also told of the existence of the rich gold mine in the mountains to the west. Since he was never allowed to visit the mine, Lucero was unable to pinpoint its exact location, but he knew the direction the Indians rode when departing for the site.

As life for Jose Lucero returned to normal in San Augustin, he often thought of returning to the Cerro de Lauriana and trying to find the gold mine. If he could locate it, he was convinced, he would become a wealthy man. Lucero grew to manhood and eventually became a contributing member of the little community, took a wife, and fathered children. All the while, he continued to dream of the fortune in gold that awaited in the mountains.

On at least four occasions, Lucero undertook expeditions into the range in search of the mine. Twice he was forced out of the mountains by Indians, and on two other trips he simply got lost.

For most of his life, Jose Lucero dreamed of the riches that he knew could be found in the elusive mine shaft. He told the story to others in the village, and once in a while some of them, using Lucero's vague directions, would try to locate the mine, but none were successful.

One of Lucero's sons, Ramon, also developed a passion for finding the gold mine of the Indians. As a young man he made dozens of trips into the mountains searching for the elusive shaft. He always came away empty-handed, but he never gave up hope of finding it.

Over the years, Ramon Lucero interviewed a number of older Indians in the region about the gold mine. Most of them acknowledged its existence and a few claimed to have actually visited it and dug out some of the gold. To tell someone outside the tribe of its location, they explained, was a transgression punishable by death.

When he was in his thirties, Ramon Lucero had a chance meeting with an elderly Indian in Santa Rosa that was to reinforce his passion for finding the gold mine. He noticed that the Indian was wearing a bracelet of hammered gold, the workmanship suggesting it was handmade by a semi-skilled artisan. Lucero asked about the bracelet, and the Indian responded that he made it himself from gold he had taken from a very old mine high up in the Cerro de Luariana! The Indian described the mine as being a short distance from a spring and one which had a very small and narrow entrance. The gold inside the mine, according to the old man, was so pure that it could be cut from the rock using only a pocketknife. Ramon told the Indian about his father being taken captive as a young boy and learning about what must be the very same gold mine.

During his conversation with the old Indian, Lucero was stunned to hear him state that he would take him to the mine! He explained that with all the time that has elapsed, most of the hostilities between the Indians and the whites has disappeared and he wasn't certain that anyone in the tribe would mind sharing the secret of the mine's location.

For the next two hours, Lucero and the Indian made preparations to hike to the gold mine. During the following week, supplies were purchased and arrangements were made. At the appointed hour, Lucero met the Indian at a pre-arranged location not far from the Cerro de Lauriana. To the Indian's dismay, Lucero brought along a partner.

The partner was a man who was familiar with the tale of the lost Indian gold mine and possessed some knowledge of geology and mining. During the time that had passed since Lucero first visited with the old Indian, the two men had entered into a legal partnership and agreed to share all of the gold they found.

The Indian did not like the arrangement and explained his misgivings to the two men. The agreement, he said, was to lead only Lucero to the mine. The two men insisted, and grudgingly the Indian set off toward the mountains, following a winding trail that switch-backed its way to the higher altitudes.

During the trek, Lucero's partner asked the old Indian a number of questions about the location of the mine, the landmarks, the thickness of the vein, and the nearest spring. The Indian responded to most of the questions, but remained somewhat vague about specific landmarks.

That evening the three men made camp. While cooking their dinner over a low campfire, Lucero and the partner continually spoke of what they were going to do with their great wealth once they converted the gold into cash. Each man dreamed of living a life of splendor. The old Indian quietly cautioned them that it was not good to speak of such things. The two white men merely laughed at the caution and continued talking about how they were going to spend their money.

During evening camp of the second day, Lucero's partner asked the old man how much farther it was to the mine. The old man explained they would reach it around noon of the following day. Before wrapping up in their bedrolls for the night, the Indian pulled Lucero aside and told him he regretted promising to lead him to the mine and wished to return to his village. Lucero assured the old man everything was going to be alright and that in just a few days they would all be rich.

It was not to happen. When Lucero and his partner rolled out of their blankets at dawn, the old Indian was gone.

For the next two days, Lucero and his partner combed the side of the mountain in search of the mine but were unable to find it or the nearby spring. Disappointed, they returned home.

For the next decade, the two men returned to the range time and again to look for the gold mine. During one trip they found a spring, located approximately two and a half day's walk from their starting point. Though they searched for the next several days around the vicinity of the spring, they were still unable to locate a mine.

Lucero often visited the place where he first met the old Indian but could never find him. When he inquired about the old man, people who knew him said they had not seen him in years, that he seemed to have just vanished.

When he was an old man, Ramon Lucero met another Indian who was wearing crudely fashioned gold ornaments. When questioned by Lucero, the Indian, like the one so many years earlier, explained the gold had come from a traditional source, an old mine located high in the Cerro de Lauriana. To the Indian, Lucero also related the story of his father's capture and of learning about the mine from the Indians. He also told of his search for the mine with the old Indian who promised to guide him.

All the while Lucero spoke, the Indian merely nodded. When Lucero explained that when he was only half a day away from finding the mine, the old Indian abandoned him and his partner and was never seen again.

The Pueblo Indian to whom Lucero spoke continued to nod his head. When Lucero mentioned the Indian who guided he and his partner into the mountains, the Pueblo replied that he knew of it.

Surprised, Lucero asked him how he knew. The Indian explained that the mine was sacred to the Pueblo tribe and that its location was a carefully guarded tribal secret. He explained that very few

Pueblos these days knew the location of the old mine, and those that did were bound to keep the information within the tribe and never to share it with outsiders. The old Indian who led Lucero toward the mine, said the Pueblo, dishonored the covenant.

When Lucero asked what happened to the old man, the Pueblo said he was killed by members of the tribe.

Today, the older Pueblos generally refuse to speak of the secret gold mine. Some claim they have never heard of it. A few maintain it does not even exist, that is only a folktale. Others admit to having some knowledge of the mine but insist they are unaware of its location. Still others simply walk away when the subject is brought up.

*   *   *

The secret gold mine of the Pueblos is still there, according to researchers and those close to the Indians. Reputedly, the mine still contains a thick, rich vein of almost pure gold. It is rumored that some of the older Indians still travel to the mine, still dig out some of the gold on accasion, and use it to help their families.

A few of the elders have been offered large sums of money to reveal the location of the rich gold mine, but in every case they refuse. Several years ago, one of the Pueblo elders was offered $10,000 if he would lead a party of treasure hunters to the secret mine. He looked at their money and merely laughed and told them in one short afternoon he could dig that much and more from the mine.

The secret gold mine of the Pueblos is still there, high in the Cerro de Lauriana, and still eluding the searches of those who would try to find it. Whoever eventually locates this rich deposit must do so on his own initiative, for he can never expect to receive any help from the Indians.

THE LOST SANCHEZ MINES
AND BURIED TREASURES

During the late 1590s, a group of Spanish colonists, led by Juan de Onate, arrived in what was to become New Mexico and settled in an area several miles northwest of present-day Santa Fe. They named it San Gabriel, and among these early settlers was a large family named Sanchez.

Though the Sanchez family thrived in this new environment, they desired more land to expand their agricultural pursuits. They wanted to grow extensive crops of corn and hay, and they wished to establish a large apple orchard. When they approached the colony's leaders with their plan, however, they were opposed. Refusing to remain under the strict, incomprehensible guidelines of the village, the Sanchez family packed up, departed San Gabriel, and resettled in a location approximately fifty miles to the east to the new settlement of Mora, located just north of the present-day town of Las Vegas. Here, in addition to farming and ranching, the Sanchez' took up prospecting and mining the precious metals from the nearby Sangre de Cristo Mountains. According to extant Sanchez family documents, gold was found in abundance in the mountains near Mora.

Around 1610, the Sanchez clan began casting about for

new opportunities and adventures. They packed up their belongings, along with an impressive amount of gold they had accumulated from the mine, and departed Mora. A few weeks later they found a location several miles to the southwest and settled along the east flank of a small mountain range. They named this new place Manzano, the Spanish word for apple, and the granite range that loomed just to the west was called the Manzano Mountains. Here, the Sanchez family established orchards and bounteous fields of crops and prospered.

While preparing the land for vegetables, fruits, and feed for livestock, several members of the Sanchez family discovered gold in the Manzano Mountains. During the next several years as the fields and orchards became productive, it is estimated that the Sanchez family also mined millions of dollars worth of gold which they melted down and cast into ingots.

For generations, the Sanchez family worked the land and the mines, all to great profit. The gold mines in the nearby Manzano Mountains were so rich that the Sanchez', like so many others who found the rich ore in the region, captured and enslaved area Indians to perform the backbreaking labor required for digging out the ore. And, as happened with so many others, the great Pueblo Indian uprising of 1680 forced the Sanchez family to flee the area only days before the well-armed and angry Indians swept through, killing everyone they encountered. Before leaving Manazano, the Sanchez' closed down their mine and covered it up so it could not be found. They also loaded eight donkeys with heavy packs filled with gold ingots, all of which they intended to transport into Mexico as they sought safety from the vengeance-minded Pueblos. Before leaving their Manzano holdings, they also buried several more loads of gold at various locations in the apple orchard.

By the time the Sanchez' reached the little village of Quarai just a few miles south of Manazano, they realized the heavily laden donkeys would not be able to travel fast enough to outdistance the Indians. At Quarai, the Sanchez men, with the help of several priests, dug several holes on the mission grounds and buried the gold ingots.

The mission priests, once returned to Mexico, were sent back to Spain and never visited Quarai again. The Sanchez family took up residence deep in Mexico and awaited the opportunity to return to Manzano and reclaim their fields and orchards as well as their gold mine. The chance came in 1692 when the region was subsequently reconquered by the Spaniard De Vargas who, with a large mounted force, subdued the Indians once again.

Gradually, a few members of the Sanchez family returned, but most decided to remain in Mexico rather than take the chance of facing another Indian uprising. One of the descendants, a man named Eugenio Sanchez, set about to find the gold buried at Manazano on his return. Though Eugenio helped to bury the gold before the hasty retreat from the Indian uprising years earlier, he had difficulty remembering the exact locations of the caches. Presently, however, he did find one of them.

After digging up the gold, Eugenio set some of it aside as living expenses, then reburied the greatest portion of it back in the orchard. Soon afterward, he died without telling any of his children where it was located.

Outside of the Sanchez family, very little was known about the rich gold mine in the Manzano Mountains. Though some of the descendants, resorting to vague directions that were hastily scribbled out years earlier, tried to find the mine but they were never successful.

Then, in 1956, a man from Mountainair, some ten miles southeast of the Manzano Mountains, found the mine. He came to the range to hunt deer, and as he was following a

trail high on the west side of the range, he found a partially covered entrance to an old mine. Clearing away some
of the rubble that was piled at the opening, he entered.
Several yards into the mine he encountered a vertical
shaft. Leading down into the darkness below was an old,
cracked rawhide ladder. Though the deer hunter was
tempted to descend the unsafe ladder to learn what might
be found at the bottom, his better judgment kept him from
it. Instead, he decided to return to Mountainair, purchase
a stout rope, and return to the mine and explore it further.

When he returned to the area several days later, the
deer hunter was unable to relocate the opening to the
shaft. He searched for days, but was never able to find it.
He came back to the mountains many times during the
next fourteen years in hopes of encountering the shaft, but
with no success. Researchers of Sanchez family history in
this area are convinced the deer hunter accidentally stumbled onto the old Sanchez Mine. Had the finder been able
to descend to the bottom of the dark shaft, he likely would
have found an amazing fortune in gold ore.

*　　　*　　　*

Yet another man is given credit for finding, and then
losing, what was most likely the Lost Sanchez gold mine.
This man, a prospector and miner, found an old, partially
covered shaft that matched the description of the one
found by the deer hunter years earlier. The prospector
claimed the mine was located on the west slope of the
Manzano Mountains not far from the crest of the ridge.
The shaft itself is located between two large pine trees and
lies within a dense stand of forest. Before he was able to
pursue his interest in the old mine, the prospector passed
away.

*　　　*　　　*

In 1969, the mine was apparently found once again. Like the others before him, the finder was never able to make his way back to it.

A man named Peter Talifierro was prospecting along the western slope of the Manzano Mountains near the summit when he chanced upon the opening to what he described as a very old mine shaft. Fashioning a torch from some pine limbs that were rich in pitch, he entered the shaft, proceeded to explore along its length, and soon discovered a vertical drop of what he estimated to be approximately sixty feet. Attached to metal spikes that had been hammered into the wall next to him was an old rawhide ladder. Afraid of placing his weight on the rotten ladder, Talifierro decided to return to his home in Albuquerque, purchase a new rope ladder, and return to the mountains at the first opportunity.

Several weeks passed before Talifierro could make the trip back to the Manazano Mountains. When he did, he brought a carbide lamp, two flashlights, and a 100-foot rope ladder. After attaching the ladder to the metal spikes, Talifierro descended into the vertical shaft.

What he found at the bottom astounded him, he reported later. The shaft ended in a sizeable room, one large enough for him to stand at full height. Pointing a flashlight at one wall of the room, Talifierro gazed upon a three foot thick vein of gold-laced quartz. The gold was so pure that he could easily cut it out of the rock with the point of his penknife.

And so he did. For the next hour-and-a-half, Talifierro removed enough gold to fill two shirt pockets. He decided to return to Albuquerque, use the gold to purchase some supplies, and then come back to the mine as soon as possible to extract more of the rich gold.

On returning home, Talifierro shared his discovery with a friend named Barton O'Donnell. He invited O'Donnell to partner with him, the friend agreed, and Talifierro gave him vague directions to the mine.

During the next several weeks the two men began accumulating supplies and making plans for the trip back to the Manzanos. Their intention was to establish a camp near the opening of the mine and live in the range for a week to ten days at a time as they removed the gold. The two friends met often over coffee and discussed how they would spend their newfound wealth.

During the preparations for the trip, Talifierro suffered an accident while working on the roof of his home which resulted in a broken leg. The break turned out to be a particularly bad one, and it kept him hospitalized for nearly two weeks. When he returned home, Talifierro was placed in traction where he remained for several more weeks. In the meantime, O'Donnell grew impatient with waiting to travel to the mine and he backed out of the partnership.

Several weeks later when Talifierro was finally able to stand, he was forced to use a cane as he hobbled about and tried to regain the use of his leg. More weeks passed, and one day as Talifierro was climbing the stairs of his two-story house, he fell and rebroke the leg.

Pete Talifierro was never able to regain his mobility again and was forced to move about in a wheelchair. On at least two occasions, he tried to enlist another partner to mine the gold for a share. When Talifierro related the story of his discovery of the rich gold mine in the Manzano Mountains, however, no one believed him. As far as is known, when Pete Tolliver died he took with him the secret to the location of the Lost Sanchez Mine.

*   *   *

The Lost Sanchez Mine of the Manazano Mountains remains lost today, as does the fortunes in gold buried in the old apple orchard and the eight donkey loads of gold ingots buried on the grounds near the ruins of the old Quarai mission.

The tale of the lost fortunes of the Sanchez family do not end with the Manazano experience. The original highly productive gold mine in the Sangre de Cristo Mountains was actually found, mined to great profit by a settler in the region, then lost once again.

During the late 1850s, a German immigrant named Frank Metzgar settled near the town of Mora. A bachelor, Metzgar established a fairly successful cattle ranch which supplied beef for the solders at nearby Fort Union. He also opened a trading post that did good business with travelers, miners, and soldiers. Before long, Metzgar had accumulated 8,000 acres of land.

Within a short time after opening the trading post, Metzgar married Viviana Martinez, the daughter of a prominent family and a widow with five children. In time, the two had several more children of their own.

Metzgar eventually added sheep to his ranching enterprises and hired a number of competent Mexican herders to look after them. One afternoon while tending a flock of sheep in the foothills of the Sangre de Cristo Mountains not far from the tiny settlement of Cleveland, one of the sheep herders fell through a concealed opening and landed several feet below in a deep hole. On regaining his composure, the herder discovered he was at the bottom of a mine shaft and was unable to climb out. Looking around, he found several old mining tools in the shaft.

For most of the afternoon he called out for help. By evening, another herder came out to take his turn with the flock, found the first herder missing, and heard his cries. A dead pine log was placed in the hole and the herder was able to crawl out.

The next morning, the second herder related the incident to Meztgar who hurried out to the shaft to see what lay inside. After examining the old shaft closely, Metzgar discovered a seam of rich gold. He lost no time in establishing a mining operation of his own, and within a few weeks the gold mine was provding him with a profit that far exceeded his ranching activities. Researchers are convinced that Frank Metzgar had reopened the original Lost Sanchez Mine.

While Metzgar involved his children and stepchildren in the daily operations of the ranch and trading post, he remained very secretive about the gold mine. Not only did he not reveal the location to them, he never revealed how much gold was taken from it and how much money he realized from the operation. The nearest bank was in Santa Fe, fifty miles to the southwest over difficult roads. Rather than trust his fortune to a bank, however, Metzgar buried it somewhere on his property.

During the first decade of the twentieth century, Frank Metzgar was an old man and in very poor heath. Eventually, he was confined to his bed at his ranch house, his family standing vigil over the fading husband and father.

Frank Metzgar decided that before dying he needed to reveal to his family the locations of the rich gold mine and the numerous caches of buried gold on the property.

One evening the old patriarch called his family to his bedside and told them about the existence of the mine. He also related that he had buried several trunkloads of gold at several different locations on the property. In addition, he said, he filled several pairs of old worn out boots with coins he'd saved over the years and buried them here and there on the grounds.

Just as he was about to provide details relative to all of the hiding places, visitors dropped in to pay a call to the sick man. Metzgar said he preferred not to discuss his wealth with guests in the house and he would wait until they departed. Later, when the family finally bid the visitors goodnight and returned to Metzgar's bedside, they found the old man dead.

*   *   *

In 1900, a rancher named James Schumaker leased a large portion of the old Metzgar holdings. While living on the old ranch, Schumaker heard a number of tales about the old man's lost mine and buried gold.

One summer afternoon during a drought, Schumaker was riding around the ranch checking on the water levels in the streams and ponds. He paused at one of the ponds that was quite low and saw something odd out in the middle of it. It appeared to be a wooden chest. Wading out in to the shallow water, Schumaker pulled the old chest from the muck of the bottom, carried it to the shore, and broke it open. Inside, he found several gold ingots which eventually brought him nearly $70,000 when he sold them.

Convinced of the truth of Frank Metzgar's lost mine and buried treasures, Schumaker spent several more years on the ranch searching for treasure, but he never found any.

*   *   *

It would be impossible to estimate the value of the gold buried by the Sanchez family and Frank Metzgar in the various locations. It is likewise impossible to estimate the value of the gold that still, presumably, resides in the lost mines in the Sangre de Cristo and Manzano Mountains. It would be safe to guess, however, that it would be in the tens of millions of dollars.

SOUTHEAST

CABALLO MOUNTAINS TREASURE

New Mexico's Caballo Mountains lie just to the south and somewhat east of Truth or Consequences. This range, though not particularly extensive, is known for its extremely rugged landscape. It is also home to rattlesnakes, scorpions, tarantulas, and mountain lions. For centuries it served as a hiding place for warring Indians, the location being entirely defensible and one the United States cavalry entered with the utmost caution. Between the Civil War and the beginning of the twentieth century, the Caballo Mountains were a favored retreat for outlaws.

During the past four centuries, accounts of lost mines and buried Spanish treasures hidden deep in the Caballo Mountains have endured and prospered. Indeed, centuries-old gold ingots have been found in the Caballos in abundance, and tales abound about the thousands of bars that were left behind. The following is one such story.

*   *   *

During the first few decades of the 1900s, many of the residents of Hot Springs (now called Truth or Consequences) were well acquainted with accounts of lost Spanish treasure located somewhere deep in the Caballo

Mountains. On a weekly basis, a number of treasure hunters, both amateur and professional, could be spotted walking the environs of the range in search of the gold they knew was hidden in the range. In fact, several of the Hot Springs citizens moved to this growing settlement solely to be closer to the trove they were certain awaited discovery by one of them.

One April day in 1929, a tall, lean man named Willie Daught drove an old beat up pick-up truck onto the Hilton Ranch located near the foothills of the Caballo Mountains. Daught met with the foreman and arranged to stay for a few weeks in the bunkhouse and take meals in exchange for a modest fee. In addition, Daught leased a horse and saddle from the foreman.

Daught was a quiet man and tended to keep to himself. He was rarely seen around the ranch save for those times he came to dine with the hired hands. On most mornings just after breakfast, Daught was seen riding the winding trail that led from the ranch into the Caballo Mountains. He carried only a full canteen and some digging tools.

One morning the foreman encountered Daught as he was saddling the horse and asked him what he was looking for in the mountains. Daught remained evasive and directed the conversation elsewhere.

The foreman also noticed that Daught often carried a piece of rolled leather under one arm. When he inquired about it, Daught unrolled it and showed him, the foreman recalled years later, a crude map indicating peaks, trails, springs, and other recognizable Caballo Mountain landmarks. At a certain place on the map there was a notation that allegedly pointed the way to a large trove of gold ingots buried by early Spanish miners. Daught said he found the old map one day while digging around the ruins of old Fort Seldon.

The foreman noted that each evening when Daught returned from the mountains he was dirty and exhausted. He would clean up for supper, then return to the bunkhouse without saying much of anything save for greeting and gratitude.

One afternoon Daught rode into the ranch and asked the foreman if he could visit with him for a few minutes. The foreman invited Daught into the main house. Daught was visibly excited, and once the two men were seated, he pulled from his canvas pack a thick, heavy bar approximately ten inches long. After handing it to the foreman, he explained that it was gold, that it was centuries old, and that it was part of a Spanish treasure trove he found in the mountains that morning. Daught also told the foreman that he was holding only half of the bar—the original was so heavy he was unable to carry it with ease so he cut it in half. Daught said the bar was only one of a total of 1,465 he found in a cave in the Caballlo Mountains!

During the next few days while living at the Hilton Ranch, Daught provided the foreman with a number of specifics relative to the location of the treasure. He said it was hidden in a very ancient mine shaft, the entrance to which was very obscure. Nearby, he said, grew a large bush with red berries. Not far from the bush was a "big cactus." Several yards from the entrance to the mine was a small spring that provided a bare trickle of water. Just inside the shaft, Daught found the remains of an old arrastre and forge, and just beyond these items he encountered five skeletons. The mine, he said, was approximately 400 yards up the slope from the ruins of an old stone house.

The day after showing the portion of the gold ingot to the foreman, Willie Daught departed the Hilton Ranch for Las Cruces to sell it. Little did he know that the news of his discovery was, at that moment, spreading throughout this part of the southwest like a desert wind, and the news only served to anger some of those who had spent many years trying to locate the gold. Unknown to Daught, he was followed as he made his way from the ranch toward Las Cruces.

On the way to Las Cruces, Daught stopped for the night in Hatch where he had some business to conduct and checked into a hotel. That night as he was preparing for sleep, three men burst into his room, attacked him, and beat him unconscious. Daught awoke two hours later in the back of a pick-up truck on his way to the Caballo Mountains. His hands and feet were bound tightly with rope.

Once in the mountain range, the three men demanded Daught reveal the location of the treasure trove. When he refused, they beat him more, and for the next two days subjected him to horrible tortures. On the third night of his ordeal, Daught managed to escape from his captors while they were sleeping and fled back to the Hilton Ranch.

Within a month, Daught formed a partnership with a man named Buster Ward. He showed Ward the location of the treasure, and together the two men removed a number of the heavy gold ingots, carried them out of the range, and placed them in the trunk of Ward's car. The partners intended to travel to Douglas, Arizona, and sell the gold to a contact with whom Ward had done business in the past.

On the highway to Douglas, Ward's car was forced off the road by another, and the two men were held at gun-point while they were robbed of the gold bars. Daugth recognized the robbers as the same three men who had abducted him weeks earlier.

During the next three months, the pair managed to exchange a number of the gold ingots for cash, but it soon became clear they were being watched and followed. Despite the continual setbacks and threats to their lives,

Daught and Ward managed to sell around $750,000 worth of the gold.

Then one day Willie Daught and Buster Ward simply disappeared. Ward's car was found out in the desert near Hatch several yards from a seldom used dirt road. None of the contents of the vehicle had been taken and there was no evidence of foul play. Willie Daught never returned to the room he was renting in Truth or Consequences and none of his belongings—clothes, tools, and a camera—had been removed. Most people were convinced that Daught and Ward were murdered because of their knowledge of the location of the lost Spanish treasure. If so, it is a murder that remains unsolved to this day.

The owner of the Hilton Ranch, a man named Holden, searched for the old mine and the treasure for several years. Using the information that Daught provided the foreman, Rancher Holden spent days at a time exploring the Caballo Mountain range and looking for the berry bush, the big cactus, and the small spring, but all for naught.

During the 1950s, a party of deer hunters came upon a man lying in a ravine in the foothills of the Caballo Mountains. The stranger was near death as a result of thirst, exposure, and a festering rattlesnake bite. While he babbled incoherently, the stranger clutched tightly to a ragged old pack at his side. The hunters transported him to the hospital in Truth or Consequences where he was treated for dehydration and the snake bite. As a matter of routine, the police were called and a report made. The stranger was unable to communicate effectively, so the policemen searched through his belongings in an attempt to find some identification. Finding none in his pants or jacket, they turned their attention to his pack and were surprised to discover a single, large, heavy gold ingot.

For the next three days, the delirious man was questioned as to his identity and the origin of the gold bar. He mumbled cryptic references to thousands of gold bars he found in a mine shaft someplace in the Caballo Mountains but revealed nothing about the exact location. On the morning of the fourth day, he was dead.

*   *   *

There are numerous other accounts of gold ingots, as well as golden church artifacts, being found in the Caballo Mountains. Whether they are from the same location where Willie Daught found his or from others, no one knows for certain.

The Caballo Mountains remain one of the most intriguing sites on the North American continent for lost treasure. It continues to claim the attention of treasure hunters, and on any given afternoon individuals and parties of hopeful men still explore the rugged fastness of this curious range.

CHATO'S TREASURE

Outside of his ten year career as a highwayman, little is known about Pedro "Chato" Nevarez. His image is wrapped up in folklore and legend, and he is regarded as one of New Mexico's earliest outlaws. Some researchers claim Nevarez was an Indian, probably Apache. Others maintain he was a Mexican. Some say he was a half-breed. The truth of Nevarez' origins will likely never be known, but the fact remains that he was the leader of a gang that preyed on travelers and supply trains moving north and south along the Rio Grande Valley between Mesilla and Hot Springs, now called Truth or Consequences.

Nevarez received his nickname, Chato, as a result of a wound. Chato mean "snub-nosed," and according to legend, a portion of his nose had been sliced off during a knife fight.

Nevarez has been described as bloodthirsty and given to the slow and sadistic torture of prisoners he would occasionally take. Between the years 1639 and 1649, few were safe along the route that paralleled the Rio Grande.

The historical record shows that Nevarez and his gang, composed primarily of Pueblo and Apache Indians as well as some Mexicans, preferred to attack caravans coming out of Mexico and carrying supplies—food, mining equipment, guns, and ammunition—all destined for the Spanish settlements along the river. Such pack trains were generally unescorted by soldiers and were easy victims for Nevarez.

Following each raid, Nevarez and his gang would retreat to their hideaway deep in remote Soledad Canyon in the Organ Mountains.

*   *   *

One of Chato Nevarez' last raids took place during April 1649. From hiding, the outlaw and his gang watched the advance of a northbound pack train led by monks. The train left the monastery at Alcoman, located some forty miles north of Mexico City, months earlier and was distributing church items along with some silver coins to the various missions located in the Rio Grande river valley.

It was almost sundown when the monks decided to stop for the day and make camp. They led the pack train to a wooded location near the river and were gathering firewood when Nevarez and his men swooped down upon them from a nearby low ridge. The attack was met with no resistance -- The monks were unarmed and were of the Augustinian Order which preached non-violence.

The heavily laden pack mules were quickly rounded up and herded away toward the east. After traveling approximately two miles, Nevarez called a halt and he and his men dismounted and tore open the packs. Inside they found a number of chalices, candlesticks, crucifixes, and other church-related items, all made of gold. In addition, they discovered several of the packs were filled with silver coins.

Nevarez ordered a portion of the loot divided among his men on the spot. The remainder was to be taken to the hideout in Soledad Canyon and cached in a nearby cave.

In the meantime, the monks returned to El Paso del Norte where they sent a report of the robbery via messenger to church officials at Alcoman. Several weeks later, a contingent of armed and mounted soldiers, all dressed as monks and leading a pack train, arrived in El Paso, conferred with the missionaries, and then proceeded northward. The intent of the soldiers was to entice the highwaymen to attack the faux pack train and capture or kill them.

Perceiving this new caravan as yet another easy robbery, Nevarez and his men charged out of an arroyo and were among their intended victims when the soldiers threw back their robes and brought forth their weapons. The ensuing fight was brief, but the element of surprise favored the soldiers. Within minutes, several on each side were killed but the outlaws were solidly defeated. Those not slain during the fight were taken prisoner, among them Nevarez. All of the bandits were roped together and made to walk the entire distance to Alcoman.

Months later, Chato Nevarez and his surviving companions were tried and sentenced to die on the gallows. As he lived out his final days in a dingy cell, Nevarez attempted to buy his way out of prison. Befriending one of the guards, the outlaw promised to pay him a fortune in gold and silver from his treasure cache in the Organ Mountains located far to the north. During this exchange, Nevarez' description of the location of the treasure cave was written down by one of the monks who attended the prisoners. In spite of his efforts to bargain, however, Nevarez was hanged a week later.

*   *   *

Chato Nevarez and his outlaw activities would likely be relegated to a minor footnote in New Mexico history were it not for an event that occurred in 1930. During the summer of that year, a man brought an extremely old metal safe to an El Paso, Texas, establishment that specialized in repairing and restoring old trunks, strongboxes, and safes. The owner of the safe told the proprietor that the item came from the old monastery at Alcoman. As he was in the process of removing the deteriorated interior wall of the safe, the proprietor found an aged manuscript that had been hidden between the inner lining and the outer wall. Several weeks later, the manuscript was sent to a language expert at the University of Texas in Austin for translation. It turned out to be the description of Chato Nevarez' treasure cave as it was written down by an Alcoman monk nearly three centuries earier!

The translation reads:

> Go to El Paso del Norte and inquire where the Organ Mountains are. The mountains are located up the river two days travel from El Paso del Norte by horseback. It is a large mountain range with some peaks on it. You will find in these mountains two gaps. One is called Tortuga and the other is called Soledad. Before entering the first gap turn to your right and go to about the middle of the slope of the mountain where you will find a verythick juniper tree. From this tree proceed downhill 100 paces to a spot covered with small stones. Look for a blue stone a great deal larger than the others. A cross was made on this stone by a chisel. Remove this slab and dig about a man's height and you will find a hole full of silver taken from the packs of six mules. You will find at the bottom of this hole some boards. Remove the boards and you will find coins from three mule trains we captured and buried there. Following this go to Soledad Canyon and follow up the pass until you reach a very large spring which is the source of the water which

runs through the canyon. The spring is covered with cattails.

Proceed to the right to about the middle of the slope of the mountains. Look with great care for three juniper trees which are very thick and set not very far apart. In front of these trees is a small precipice in which can be found a large flat rock on which a cross has been carved with a chisel. Between the trees and the rock exists a mine which belonged to a wealthy Spaniard named Jorge Colon. The mine is so rich that the silver ore can be cut with a knife. The opening of the mine is covered by a large door we constructed from the timbers of the juniper. On top of this door is placed a large red rock. It will take 25 men to remove this rock. Just inside the door can be found gold crucifixes, images, platters, vases, and other items.

Passing this, continue down into the mine shaft and you will encounter a tall stack of silver bars. Beyond this lies mining equipment. Thousands of families will be benefited by this wealth.

About two years following the translation of this document, yet another one containing a description of the location of the treasure was discovered. Apparently, during the surprise attack by the soldiers on Nevarez' gang, one of the highwaymen was wounded but managed to escape and hide. Bleeding badly, he was discovered two days later lying on the front steps of the mission at Dona Ana. The outlaw lived another day but before he died he confessed his sins to the priest and told him where the valuables taken from previous robberies were hidden. The priest wrote down the description, but attributing it to the ravings of a dying man, he thought little of it and filed it with other mission documents. Several weeks later, the priest wrote a letter to the head of the Alcoman monastery in

Mexico relating what the dying man had told him. He set the letter aside intending to mail it soon, but mission obligations directed his attentions elsewhere.

During the autumn of 1879, the Dona Ana mission was attacked and looted by the Apache raider Victorio. After ransacking the church and stealing the golden and silver religious icons, Victorio raided the storehouses and residences taking food and supplies. Books, letters, and documents were scattered. Among the papers retrieved the following day was the letter written by the priest, the one that contained the dying bandit's description of the treasure cache. In part, the letter read:

In Soldead Canyon there is a natural cave in the brow of a hill opening toward the south. There is a cross cut into the rock above the entrance to the cave and directly in front of a young juniper tree. For better directions, there are three medium-sized peaks toward the rising sun whose shadows converge in the morning 250 paces east of the cave entrance and a little to the south. Two hundred and fifty paces from this point directly north can be found an embankment from where by looking straight ahead you can see the Jornada del Muerto as far as the eye can see. The distance from this point to the cave should be exactly the same as the distance to the place where the shadows of the peaks converge. One hundred paces from the entrance to the cave down the arroyo you will find a dripping spring. The entrance to the cave has been covered to the depth of a man's height and ten paces beyond the entrance there is an adobe wall which must be torn down in order to gain access. At the bottom of a long tunnel the cave separates into two parts: The left cave contains two mule-loads worth of coined silver and the right cave contains golden candlesticks, images, and crucifixes taken in a robbery.

In 1913, a miner named Ben Brown was hunting in the mountains one day when he made an amazing discovery. Brown shot a deer but only wounded it. The animal bounded away and Brown followed its trail for 300 yards before finally losing it. Exhausted, the hunter sat in the shade of a large juniper tree while he caught his breath. From this vantage point on a slope, Brown scanned the area hoping to find the wounded deer but noticed something else.

Not far away on the same hillside Brown spotted an area that appeared to be filled in with rocks. Based on his lifelong career as a miner, he knew this was not a natural occurrence and wondered why someone would go to the trouble to move tons of rock for this purpose.

Brown walked over to the site and examined it. As he did so, he began recalling the tale of Pedro Nevarez' Soledad Canyon treasure. At the site, Brown noticed the three conical peaks alluded to in Nevarez' statement. From the juniper under which he had sat, he walked 250 paces in the direction of the rising sun, then north for the same distance. Here he found himself on a low ridge overlooking the Jornada del Muerto, the so-called Journey of Death, a vast, arid plain that extended far to the west Returning to the juniper tree, Brown walked downhill 100 paces and stopped in an arroyo where the dripping spring was supposed to be located, but he found no sign of it. On a hunch, Brown dug into the sandy bottom of the arroyo and found water six inches below the surface.

Before the sun rose the next morning, Brown was back at the site with some digging tools. Patiently, he sat and watched the shadows of the three peaks until they converged around mid-morning. He marked the spot with a cairn of rocks, then strode 250 paces to the west. At the point where he stopped, he found a great deal of rock and debris filling what appeared to be a cave. Based on the description in the legend, Brown was convinced he had located the treasure cache of Chato Nevarez.

Brown immediately undertook the task of removing the rubble. After working for nearly two hours he was six feet down in the vertical opening when he encountered a large flat stone. On the surface of the stone an image of a crucifix had been scratched.

By this time, Brown was exhausted from the grueling work and decided to stop for the day. He covered the image of the crucifix with dirt before leaving the site and returning to his home in Las Cruces.

As soon as the county clerk's office opened, Brown filed a mining claim on the site he found. Before the day was over, he had loaded his vehicle with camping gear and more excavation tools, and returned to the location. After setting up camp, he cut down the identifying juniper tree in case anyone else might be searching for the treasure.

It took most of the following day, but Brown finally succeeded in removing the large flat rock that sealed the entrance to the cave. To his utter dismay, he discovered that the cave below had also been filled with stones and soil.

For the next several days, Brown lowered himself into the excavation and removed the fill bucketful by bucketful. After digging out about twelve feet, the vertical entrance sloped and eventually leveled out into a smaller passageway through which Brown was forced to crawl. Digging out the dirt and carrying the buckets to the surface was grueling work. Then, one afternoon Brown found a Spanish coin in the dirt. It was dated 1635, and the discovery gave Brown more reason to continue.

Ten days after he began digging, Brown finally came to the adobe wall mentioned in the description by the wounded bandit. Wielding a heavy crowbar, he chopped away at it until it was demolished. Beyond the wall, the cave was open for approximately ten yards. After crawling through it, Brown came to a chamber where he was able to barely stand. Beyond the chamber he saw where the cave continued, but to his great disappointment he also saw that it was filled with dirt.

For weeks, Brown continued with the excavation process. One day among the debris he was removing he found a pick-axe. Weeks later, he shipped the tool to the Chicago Field Museum of Natural History for identification and learned that it was made of hand-forged steel and likely manufactured in Spain during the sixteenth century!

From time to time, Brown was forced to abandon his work at the treasure site to attend to his own mining operations elsewhere in the Organ Mountains. For more than a year he continued to remove dirt one bucket at a time from the cave and was growing more and more discouraged. To add to his troubles, Brown's active mines were losing money and he was forced to take a job in Las Cruces in order to provide some income. For the next few years Brown worked at other mining claims, as a forest ranger, and even as a musician. On those rare occasions when he could find the time, he would return to the treasure site and remove more of the fill.

Twenty years passed and Brown was still working at the treasure cave. He eventually took into his confidence a college professor named Campa from the University of Denver who was also keenly interested in the treasure of Pedro Nevarez. Surprisingly, Brown revealed to the professor that the treasure was not in Soledad Canyon in the Organ Mountains, but rather in a canyon bearing the same name found in the Dona Ana range some fifteen miles west!

On one occasion, Brown took the professor to the excavation. Of the cave, Campa wrote:

> *The tunnel against the hillside had the appearance of a natural cave, very similar to the subterranean formations associated with Carlsbad Caverns, except there was no moisture and the floor was covered with topsoil. For a short distance we walked upright; then we stopped and began crawling on all fours. About 200 feet down into the earth we came upon a point where the cave split into a Y going in two directions. I took one side and Ben followed the other. This was as far as he had cleared but I could see the passage continued indefinitely. Back at the surface, Ben pointed out the landmarks of the three peaks, the jornada, and the spring.*

Brown told the professor that he was trying to secure some financial backing in order to purchase expensive equipment that would facilitate the excavation process. Brown never got the backing, and around this time his other mining interests were earning him significant profits and demanded his attention.

When he could find the time, Brown continued excavating the dirt from the cave. One day, Professor Campa received a letter from Brown which conveyed some excitement about Chato's treasure. In the letter, Brown invited Campa to come to the site so he could show him what he discovered. Because of a number of university obligations, however, Campa was unable to go. A few months later he learned that Brown had died. Subsequent investigation revealed that Brown kept the location of the treasure cave from his wife and two children. A search through his belongings failed to yield a map or description of the location of the mine and the hidden treasures.

Did Ben Brown finally reach the incredible treasure cache of Chato Nevarez? If he did, he carried the secret with him to his grave.

LOST SPANISH GOLD MINE IN THE ORGAN MOUNTAINS

Demetrio Varela was born into poverty in 1824. He was one of twelve children whose family labored long and hard trying to coax food crops from the fertile floodplain of the Rio Grande not far from the present-day city of Las Cruces.

When he was only four years old there was not enough food for the large family so Demetrio and several brothers and sisters were sent to live with relatives several miles away. Things were not much better at Demetrio's new home, so by the time he was ten years old he found himself working as a laborer in the mines to the north. Though his wages were small, Demetrio enjoyed the hard work and managed to send a little money home to his family at every opportunity.

After nearly thirty years of working in the mines, Demetrio was finally able to return to the family farm. He soon grew bored, however, with coaxing corn and beans from the soil and began looking around for other opportunities to make a living. He eventually found employment riding with a rastreador, a man hired to locate lost or stolen livestock and return them to the owner. Demetrio, now about forty years old, quickly earned a reputation as a competent and dependable rastreador. His skill and competence eventually helped him land the position of foreman of a large ranch near Las Cruces owned by a widow named Dona Chonita.

Under Demetrio's management, the ranch prospered, and during the next few years the cattle herd and land holdings increased. Prosperous times were not to last, however, for during the early 1870s, a severe drought struck the region. With far less than adequate graze the cattle herd was reduced, ranch hands were let go, and soon Dona Chonita's only employee was Demetrio, and even he was seldom paid. Demetrio was considering returning to work in the mines when one cold January day he received an offer of work from a nearby rancher named Armijo.

Armijo, who had not been devastated by the drought as badly as Dona Chonita, had a number of prize cattle stolen and wanted Demetrio to find them. Demetrio went to work for Armijo the following day.

By the time Demetrio picked up the tracks of the cattle thieves, they already had a two-day head start. Accompanied by two of Armijo's ranch hands, he set out in pursuit of the thieves.

Within only a few hours on the trail of the rustlers, Demetrio noted the temperature dropping rapidly and the wind beginning to blow hard from the northwest. The riders pulled their hats low and their ponchos tighter as flakes of snow began to fall.

Around noon of the following day, Demetrio and his companions found the stolen cattle—they had been slaughtered, butchered, and the meat apparently loaded onto burros and carried away. Examining the tracks, Demetrio determined the pack train had headed to the northeast toward San Augustin Pass in the Organ Mountains.

Demetrio had heard of cattle thieves trading meat to the Indians in exchange for furs and he deduced this was the motivation for the theft. If they rode hard, Demetrio told his companions, they would stand a chance of overtaking the thieves around noon of the following day.

As the trackers followed the trail, the temperature continued to drop and the wind swirled and gusted across the desert floor ever stronger. The outline of the Organ Mountains loomed in the distance as heavy snow began falling. By the time they reached the slope leading up to San Augustin Pass, the three men were riding through a blizzard so thick it was impeding their progress.

Deciding it would be impossible to continue in the storm, Demetrio looked around for a place to take shelter. Followed by his companions, he left the trail and rode into a narrow canyon on the west side of the Organ range. Here, they took shelter under an extensive overhanging rock ledge near a copse of oak trees. After tending to their tired horses, the men gathered firewood and soon had a small blaze going. As heavy snow continued to fall, the three heated tortillas and brewed coffee over the fire and made plans to wait out the storm.

Following a short nap next to the warm fire, Demetrio awoke, stretched his tired muscles, and walked out to the grove of trees to gather more firewood. On returning, he decided to explore along the sheltered area of the rock overhang. Several yards from the campfire, he came upon a pile of rock that appeared to have been purposely stacked against the face of the cliff. Looking closer, Demetrio saw that it only partially covered a small opening into the rock wall.

Curious, Demetrio began pulling the rocks away and found an opening just wide enough to allow passage. He called to his friends about his discovery, but they indicated they preferred warming themselves by the fire.

Cautiously, Demetrio wriggled his way into the opening and crawled another twenty feet before reaching a chamber large enough to allow him to stand. He lit a tallow candle he pulled from a pocket and looked around. The first thing he noticed were thick, hand-hewn timber supports, suggesting that he was in a mine, a very old one.

Because the flickering glow of the small candle did not penetrate very far into the darkness of the chamber, Demetrio moved slowly, occasionally slipping on the wet floor or tripping over rocks that had fallen from the ceiling. As he explored, he wondered who might have operated a mine here, how long ago, and what sort of mineral had they excavated.

In the distance just beyond the light of the candle, Demetrio discerned a shape nearly shoulder high and against the far wall of the chamber. Fearing it might be a bear, he pulled his pistol from the holster and slowly approached.

As he neared the shape, the light from the candle revealed that it was only a pile of leather packs that had been stacked against the wall. An inch-thick layer of dust had accumulated on the pile. After replacing his pistol in the holster, Demetrio opened one of the sacks.

Spilling out onto the chamber floor were several small pieces of quartz laced thickly with rich gold. More sacks were opened and each one was found to contain more of the gold. Demetrio's heart thudded wildly in his chest as he contemplated the incredible fortune that lay before him.

After placing several of the gold-laced rocks in his pocket, Demetrio continued exploring the chamber. Several paces away he came upon a knee-high stack of gold ingots, perhaps 100 in all. He hefted one and stuffed it into his shirt. Not far from the gold ingots he found the remains of an old forge along with an ore crusher.

Demetrio looked for and found a place to sit down and ponder his discovery. He considered how this great wealth would help Dona Chonita save her cattle ranch. He also thought about how he would now be able to provide for his family.

As the candle burned low Demetrio realized the time had come for him to leave the shaft. When he finally crawled out of the small opening, he saw that his companions had constructed a crude shelter of limbs and pine boughs to further protect them from the blowing snow. The stack of firewood had been sufficiently added to by his companions and an inviting blaze warmed this little section of the shelter.

When his friends asked him what he found in the cave, Demetrio, deciding to keep the knowledge of the gold to himself, replied he was only looking at rock formations. He squatted by the fire, poured himself a cup of coffee, and pondered the future.

Because of the lead the cattle thieves had accumulated, and because the snowstorm continued to rage, Demetrio thought it prudent to return to the Armijo Ranch where he expressed regret to the owner that they had failed in their mission.

Riding back to Dona Chonita's ranch, Demetrio determined that he would return to the old abandoned mine in the spring and retrieve the gold to share with Dona Chonita and his family.

During the second week of March, Demetrio was visited by two old friends from the mines. They told him they had filed a mining claim near Sierra Blanca, Texas, several days ride to the southeast, and wanted Demetrio to accompany them and help with the initial excavation. Demetrio decided to go and told Dona Chonita he would return in about two months.

During the second week at the mining claim, Demetrio was preparing some dynamite to enlarge an opening to a shaft when it went off prematurely, the explosion sending pieces of shattered granite into his eyes. He was carried by wagon to a hospital at El Paso, a three-day journey, but there was nothing the doctors could do to save his sight.

As he lay recovering in the hospital, Demetrio thought constantly of the gold he found in the Organ Mountains and he wondered if he would ever be able to find it again.

Two weeks later, Dona Chonita arrived to take Demetrio back to the ranch. As he adjusted to his blindness, Demetrio spent many long hours seated on the front porch of the ranch house thinking of the gold, thinking of the fortune awaiting him in the old abandoned mine near San Augustin Pass.

Dona Chonita continued to care for Demetrio, but when she died three years later he was sent to live with a nephew in El Paso.

Practically helpless, Demetrio spent most of his time seated in the sun on his nephew's patio. With the passage of several more years, Demetrio came to the realization he would likely never return to the lost mine and retrieve the fortune in gold that awaited there, so he began telling his story to others.

Word of Demetrio's lost gold circulated throughout the southwest and elsewhere. A few months later, Demetrio, now an old man, was approached by a group of adventurers who came to New Mexico from Tennessee to search for the gold. They invited Demetrio to accompany them.

Thrilled at the prospect of being involved with the rediscovery of the gold, Demetrio readily agreed. The party left the following morning and traveled to the Armijo Ranch. From there they rode on horseback along the old road that wound through San Augustin Pass in search of the narrow canyon in which Demetrio and his companions took shelter that long ago day they were trailing the cattle thieves.

Demetrio told the treasure hunters he recalled riding past a large tree on the way to the canyon but no such tree could be found. In the years that passed since the discovery, the few streams in the area had modified their courses and roads had been constructed to accommodate the growing wagon traffic. Though they searched for two days, the party was unable to find the canyon described by Demetrio. After delivering the old man back to his nephew's house, the group left for Tennesse never to return.

Over the next few years, Demetrio received similar offers to accompany treasure hunters into the Organ Mountains but he refused all of them. He decided he could not bear the disappointment of not being able to find the sacks of gold and the gold ingots.

Those who have closely examined the tale of Demetrio Varela are convinced he discovered a long abandoned gold mine once worked by the Spanish, one that was likely overseen by the Catholic priests who were sent into this area during the seventeenth century. The mine, like many others, was likely abandoned in or around 1680, the time of the Pueblo Indian uprising.

Demetrio Varela died in 1916 at the age of ninety-two. He was buried in El Paso following small service attended only by a few members of his family.

VICTORIO PEAK TREASURE

Without doubt, the most amazing and incredible treasure tale ever to come out of New Mexico, if not the entire United States, is that associated with Victorio Peak, a somewhat unimposing granite pinnacle rising only about 500 feet from the desert floor in a remote section of the San Andres Mountains. This location is extraordinarily rugged and difficult to penetrate, and for the past several decades has been a part of the White Sands Missile Range and closed off by the United States government, making access illegal.

The forbidding landscape of Victorio Peak and the Hembrillo Basin is the setting for what may be the largest treasure cache in the world. It is believed by the vast majority of researchers that the extensive cave system found deep within Victorio Peak at one time contained several billion dollars worth of gold bars, gold and silver coins, jewelry, and artifacts. Much of this treasure is believed to still reside in the confines of the peak.

In addition to amounting what some refer to as an uncountable fortune, the Victorio Peak Treasure is also one of the most mysterious, its perplexing complications continuing to baffle and overwhelm any and all who come in contact with it.

*   *   *

Historical documentation, along with abundant artifactual evidence, has revealed that this region was visited by the followers of the Spanish explorer Francisco Vasquez de Coronado. It is also known that Coronado's miners explored for and found gold and silver in abundance in and near the San Andres Mountains. Throughout this region, pieces of Spanish armor, spurs, and saddle and bridle fittings are still found today.

Close on the heels of the Spanish explorers came representatives of the Catholic Church. Priests often accompanied the explorers or were subsequently sent into the newly mapped regions to establish colonies and convert the Indians they encountered to Christianity. In addition to constructing missions, the friars undertook a variety of agricultural practices, including vineyards for the manufacture of wine.

Growing crops of any kind was difficult in this extremely arid land, so living was a near-subsistence undertaking. Greater attention was given to the rich deposits of gold and silver found in the nearby mountains, and more often than not the Indians were put to work digging the ore from the mines, ore that was smelted, formed into ingots, and transported to church headquarters in far away Mexico City.

History is also quite clear on the fact that the Hembrillo Basin was often used as a retreat, a hideaway for the notorious Apache chief Victorio during the 1870s. Victorio raided settlements along the Rio Grande to the east and commonly preyed on travelers and freight wagons. For Victorio, this region was easy to defend, and few migrants, prospectors, or hunters ever visited this isolated location located east of the dreaded Jornada del Muerte, that extensive, arid plain that has reputedly claimed the lives of hundreds since the time of the Spaniards.

* * *

During the late 1700s, a Frenchman named Felipe La Rue, the son of a nobleman, joined a French monastery and vowed to live a life of poverty and denial. La Rue's tenure at the monastery was fraught with dissent and protest against the established authority -- he constantly challenged church officials and questioned religious policies. Convinced it would be in the best interest of the young, fiery monk to experience hardship, his superiors transferred him to Mexico and assigned him the drudgery of working in the fields.

In Mexico, La Rue was no happier than he was in France. As a result of constantly challenging his superiors, he was subjected to extra work and even received lashings on several occassions. The punishment only made La Rue angrier and more resistant to the doctrines and authority of the church.

As the months passed, La Rue often dreamed of journeying to the wild and unsettled lands far to the north of Mexico City, lands he had heard about from traders and miners. There, considered La Rue, he would establish a colony of his own, a settlement where the residents could live and worship as they wished without the heavy-handed rule of the church monitoring each decision and exacting tithes even from the poorest.

Late one night, La Rue gathered a small contingent of souls committed to his plan, stole a number of mules along with a substantial supply of provisions, and fled northward. After many weeks of tortuous travel through mountains and desert, the small party eventually arrived at El Paso del Norte on the south bank of the Rio Grande. Here, they replenished their supplies while La Rue made inquiries about the territory farther north.

After several more days of difficult walking, La Rue and his followers arrived at Hembrillo Basin. Here, they found a decent campsite, at least two fresh water springs, and plenty of game. Even more importantly, considered La Rue, the place was far from well-traveled roads and isolated enough that it was not likely they would be visited by anyone, especially representatives from the church who might be searching for them.

A few crops such as corn, beans, and squash were immediately planted and watered from the springs. Hunters were sent out to procure meat, and work was undertaken to construct shelters using the abundant native stone.

During a hunting trip, one of La Rue's followers discovered a thick, rich vein of gold in the peak that dominated Hembrillo Basin. La Rue assigned two of the monks to excavate the gold, but when it was discovered that the vein was far more extensive than they first believed, and that it was very rich, La Rue eventually ordered twenty-five men to the task, among them some Indians he had managed to convert in the weeks previous. Soon, a crude smelter was constructed and the gold melted down and formed into ingots. As the gold bars accumulated, they were stacked along one wall of a cave La Rue found in one side of the peak.

Three years after La Rue fled from the monastery in Mexico City, his whereabouts were finally discovered by the authorities. In addition to the dissident colony, the church officials also somehow received information about the extensive mining operations and the accumulation of a great fortune in gold. They decided the gold belonged to the church, so they organized an expeditionary force of soldiers to travel to the Hembrillo Basin, arrest La Rue, confiscate the gold, and return to Mexico City. Accompanying the soldiers was a contingent of monks who were to remain at the colony and continue mining the gold for the glory of god.

La Rue's Indian scouts informed him that a punitive expedition was approaching, and the renegade priest immediately ordered the entrances to the cave and the mine shaft covered. He also instructed his followers to deny the existence of the gold.

When the soldiers arrived, every member of the colony was taken prisoner. When La Rue was questioned about the gold, he denied any knowledge of it. He was immediately stripped and laid over a boulder and lashed repeatedly. Bleeding badly, his flesh hanging in bloody strips from his back, La Rue refused to admit to the existence of the mine. After two hours of this torture, La Rue finally died.

A number of the colonists were likewise tortured and killed, but according to church documents, not a single one revealed the location of the mine and the accumulated gold. Eventually, the surviving colonists were tied together and marched back to Mexico City to face further punishment by the church. The contingent of monks that accompanied the soldiers remained at Hembrillo Basin for several months, but unable to find any gold, finally gave up and returned to church headquarters.

During the 1870s, Mescalero Apache Chief Victorio was the scourge of the land. He would lead raids out across the Jornade del Muerte attacking wagons, churches, mail coaches, immigrants, and small towns. Following each raid, Victorio and his band returned to their hideout at Hembrillo Basin. On several occasions, prisoners were returned with them and the Apaches delighted in subjecting them to heinous tortures before killing them. Their bodies, it was said, were carried into a cave inside the nearby peak and hung from makeshift crucifixes.

On April, 7, 1880, a company of U.S Army cavalry entered Hembrillo Basin and engaged Victorio and his followers in a pitched battle. The Apaches were victorious, and the rocky prominence that dominates the center of Hembrillo Basin was thereafter referred to as Victorio Peak. Historians are convinced that Victorio and his Apaches fought hard in the defense of the region because of the incredible booty from raids they had amassed and, according to researchers, stored in the cave inside the mountain.

                              *   *   *

During the month of November 1937, a hunting party consisting of five men and one woman from the town of Hatch, located about sixty miles to the southwest, arrived at Hembrillo Basin on a deer hunting trip. While the woman remained in camp, the men fanned out across the basin in search of deer sign.

One of the hunters, Milton E. "Doc" Noss decided to try his luck at Victorio Peak and was climbing up one side of it when a light rain began to fall. Searching around for shelter, he finally made his way to a large rock under which he could wait out the rain. On arriving, he discovered a rectangular opening that seemed to lead straight down into the mountain. Unmindful of the rain, Noss peered into the shaft and saw that it had been excavated by human hands and that it was apparently very old. Deep in the hole almost at the limit of the light, Noss spotted a wooden pole with handholds carved into it.

When the rain subsided, Noss walked back too camp, arriving before the other hunters. He told the woman, his wife, Ova, what he had discovered on the peak, asked her to refrain from telling the others, and together the two made plans for a return trip to the area to investigate the mysterious opening.

Two weeks later, Doc and Ova Noss returned to Hembrillo Basin and, carrying ropes and a flashlight, climbed the steep slope to the opening. After tying the ropes off to a nearby boulder, Noss lowered himself into the dark shaft.

What Doc Noss discovered deep in the heart of Victorio Peak that afternoon has become one of the most controversial topics in American history, one that involves the discovery of wealth beyond imagination, one that led to murder, lawsuit, and the ultimate involvement of the United States Army and Air Force, the United States government, the government of the state of New Mexico, and a number of noted politicians and lawyers.

This is Noss's version of his discovery: After descending approximately sixty feet down the narrow shaft on the rope, he came to what he described as "a large room." Using his flashlight, he found on the walls of this room a number of "Indian drawings," some of which were carved into the rock, others which were painted. The enlarged shaft continued downward at a steep angle for another 125 feet where it leveled out. Following the shaft, Noss eventually arrived at a large natural cave inside the mountain, one apparently created by an earthquake eons earlier that split open the inside of the peak. Noss described this cave as large enough to accommodate a freight train and that it contained several smaller rooms along one side of it.

After a few paces into the cave, Noss stumbled over a skeleton. On inspection, he noted that the hands of the skeleton had been bound behind its back. Before leaving this room, according to Noss, he found a total of twenty-seven more skeletons, all bound and most of them secured to stakes that had been driven into the ground.

In one of the smaller rooms, Noss said he found an old

Wells Fargo chest and a stack of items including guns, swords, and jewels. Here, he also found a box that contained a number of letters, the most recent one dated 1880. Next to this stack was a large pile of rotted leather packs, each of which contained gold nuggets. Noss stated that it would take sixty mules to transport all of the gold in the packs.

Noss stuffed several of the gold coins and some jewels into his pockets. As he explored further in the main part of the cave, he chanced upon "thousands of bars of gold ingots stacked like cordwood."

Noss explored around the cave for another half hour until the batteries in his flashlight began losing power. With great effort, he returned to the surface and showed Ova the coins and jewels he recovered. When she asked why he didn't bring up any of the gold bars, he replied that they weighed about forty pounds apiece and he would have been unable to climb back out the shaft had he carried one. Ova continued to chide her husband for not bringing her an ingot, so he descended into the cave and, with difficulty, finally returned with one.

Over the next two years, Noss and his wife returned to Victorio Peak several times. In all of those trips, he retrieved a total of eighty-eight gold bars, each one weighing between forty and eighty pounds. He also brought to the surface dozens of artifacts, among them gold chalices and crosses, jewels, and coins.

On a few occasions, Doc Noss hired men to accompany him into the cave to retrieve some of the treasure. In 1963, one Benny Samaniego admitted that, after entering the cave with Noss, he saw "stacks of gold bars, skeletons, armor, old guns, and statues." He stated that the skeletons looked as if they had been tied to stakes and left in the cave to die.

On another occasion, Noss hired a boy named Benny Sedillo. On being interviewed years later, Sedillo, like Samaniego, described gold ingots stacked several feet high and spoke of how difficult it was to climb back out of the narrow shaft. Sedillo also told reporters that Noss told him he would kill him if he ever revealed the existence of the treasure cave to anyone.

Following two years of the difficult and tedious labor associated with carrying the heavy ingots and artifacts up the narrow shaft, Noss decided to make the job easier by widening the opening. He decided to use dynamite. After setting the charges, the resulting blast caused a cave-in which effectively sealed the opening and halted further recovery of the treasure within.

Discouraged, Noss began selling off some of the treasure he had accumulated in order to raise money to have the shaft reopened. To sell the treasure, he was forced to take on a partner, a man named Joe Andregg. Andregg helped Noss arrange for the distribution of much of the gold and artifacts on the black market.

During the subsequent months, Noss made several attempts to reopen the shaft, each one resulting in failure. Frustrated, Noss grew increasingly angry and often fought with Ova. A short time later, the two divorced.

On February 15, 1945, Doc Noss filed a claim on Victorio Peak while he was still attempting to widen the entrance. In 1949, Noss entered into a new partnership, this time with a man named Charley Ryan. Ryan was a well-respected miner who insisted he could open the shaft. Initially, Ryan was skeptical about Noss's tale of the treasure inside the mountain. In response, Noss showed Ryan fifty-one gold ingots that had been removed from the cave.

As the two men were moving heavy mining equipment into Hembrillo Basin, Ova Noss filed a counter claim on the peak. Eventually, a court determined that until a final decision was made neither of the two parties involved were allowed to enter the area.

Aggravated by the delay and his ex-wife's attempt at obtaining a share of the treasure, Noss fought often and bitterly with Ryan. One evening, an enraged Ryan shot Noss through the head, killing him instantly. Ryan was charged with murder but subsequently acquitted.

Years passed, And while Ova Noss maintained her Victorio Peak claim, the U.S. government expanded the boundaries of White Sands Missile Range to encompass Hembrillo Basin. From time to time Ova would hire some men and drive them to the basin to try to reach and reopen the shaft, but in each case they were escorted off the property by military officials.

For the next few years, Ova Noss wrote letters to state and federal agencies demanding her right to enter the property and work on her legal claim, but in every case she was denied permission, the reason given was that it was in violation of national security.

Ova Noss grew increasingly suspicious of the motives of the U.S. government relative to keeping her off of her claim. In 1961, she hired four men to enter Hembrillo Basin and make an attempt at entering the shaft. If they were successful, and if they retrieved any of the treasure, they were to receive a generous percentage. On October 28, the men climbed over a barbed wire fence, hiked the few miles to Victorio Peak, and were surprised to discover a team consisting of four U.S. Air Force officers and four U.S. Army enlisted men digging into the shaft. The officer immediately ordered the four trespassers escorted from the land.

On being informed of the presence of the military at her claim, Ova secured an attorney who, in turn, contacted New Mexico state officials. Queries were forwarded to one Colonel Jaffe at White Sands Missile Range, but he vehemently denied any excavation was taking place at Hembrillo Basin and he further insisted no military personnel were involved. Dissatisfied, Ova hired a prominent Kansas City attorney to take the case to the United States government.

During the discussions between Ova, her attorneys, and government officials, it was learned that a second entrance into the treasure cave had been discovered. In 1958, an Air Force Captain named Fiege and another man were exploring around Victorio Peak when they discovered a natural opening in one side of the mountain. The two men followed this natural passageway for several dozen yards when they encountered 100 gold ingots stacked against one wall. These could very well have been the same gold bars stored by Padre La Rue. It was subsequently learned that during the summer of 1961, Fiege, along with three other Air Force officers all assigned to White Sands Missile Range, were granted permission by the U.S. military to recover any treasure associated with the Noss claim!

On August 5, Fiege, his three companions, the commanding officer of White Sands Missile Range, a secret service agent, and fourteen military policemen returned to the peak. Oddly, Fiege and his companions were unable to relocate the second opening into the cave. A subsequent lie detector examination revealed Fiege was telling the truth about the entrance and the discovery of the gold ingots. As a result, the U.S government surprisingly ordered a full scale mining operation concentrated on Victorio Peak in spite of the fact that the claim was still held by Ova Noss. It was this government-sponsored mining activity that Noss's four hired men encountered.

Years later, several acquaintances of Fiege told authorities that the Colonel purposely misled his superiors about the location of the entrance to the cave. Later, accompanied by his companions, Fiege allegedly returned to the site and removed all of the ingots.

When Noss was informed that the U.S government was pirating her claim, she sent her attorneys to Santa Fe to get national authorities to halt the mining activities immediately and to honor her legal rights. During the subsequent hearings, it was discovered that the acting director of the Denver Mint had been granted a permit from Air Force Commander John G. Schinkle to dig for the Victorio Peak treasure! Jaffe, who was aware of the ongoing excavation at the peak, had obviously lied to any and all who inquired about the clandestine activities. Following all of the court presentations and legal arguments, a judge decreed that all mining operations at the peak cease immediately.

In 1963, the Geddes Mining Company of Denver, having been contracted by the Denver Mint, received government permits to begin digging into Victorio Peak during a designated period ranging from July 13, to September 17, a time when missiles were not being tested in the region. During these two months, uncountable tons of rock were scraped off the mountain in an attempt to find additional entrances to the vast treasure chamber below. None were found, and by the end of the period the peak, now torn and scarred, bore little resemblance to the natural promontory that previously existed.

The issue involving the immense treasure believed to be still be hidden inside Victorio Peak was to grow more complicated. Ova Noss continued her fight in the courts to be granted permission to enter the area and dig. In 1972, noted attorney F. Lee Bailey, accompanied by famous Watergate figure John Erlichmann along with Attorney General John Mitchell joined the fray.

According to court documents, Bailey represented "fifty

clients who knew the location of a cave with 100 tons of gold stacked within." Ova Noss was not listed as one of Bailey's claimants.

Finally, in Albuquerque on March 5, 1975, a federal judge declared that the U.S. Army had the right to deny permission to anyone relative to excavation at Victorio Peak. The army was also given the authority to make arrangements with claimants for any special exploration or excavation as it saw fit.

One such deal was finalized in 1977 when the army authorized a total of six different claimant groups a two week search. During this time, a ground radar survey was conducted, the results of which clearly revealed the existence of a large cave inside Victorio Peak precisely where Doc Noss said one was located. The radar survey also detected the shaft and its filling of rock and debris. The two weeks passed, however, without any of the six parties gaining entrance to the mysterious mountain.

*   *   *

All available evidence suggests strongly that deep within Victorio Peak is, or was, and incredible treasure consisting of Spanish gold, loot from Indian raids, and perhaps much, much more. It is also believed by many that a significant amount of this treasure has already been recovered by members of the U.S. Army and Air Force acting independently of government authority.

There is no doubt that the treasure originally existed: A number of the artifacts and gold ingots removed from the cave by Noss have been viewed and photographed. Additionally, employees of Noss who entered the cave actually saw and handled some of the treasure have signed affidavits to that effect.

Ova Noss passed away in 1972, but her family continues the legal battle to gain entrance to Victorio Peak. The

U.S. Army has sealed off the area and placed a locked gate atop the original shaft discovered by Noss.

Rumors persist that the U.S. Army continues its mining operation at Victorio Peak. In recent years, low-level independent flying surveys have photographed military vehicles and mining equipment on and adjacent to Victorio Peak. Inquiries to officials at White Sands Missile Range are routinely ignored.

How much of the original treasure still resides within the cave at Victorio Peak can only be conjectured. How deep and extensive was the role of the military and government authorities will likely never be known.

Individuals close to the excavation project at Victorio Peak have suggested that, rather then provide access to the treasure cave, much of the earth moving activity may have actually made entry more difficult.

The mystery continues.

SOUTHWEST

LAVA BEDS TREASURE

A few miles south of the city of Grants in west-central New Mexico lies a thick, extensive deposit of basalt, the rock formed from the cooling of lava. Eons ago, this region was volcanically active, and during this time great eruptions poured thick and wide streams of molten rock onto the landscape, lava that hardened within a few short days into solid rock. With the passage of millions of years, erosion from water and wind carved and sculpted the dark basalt into a series of maze-like canyons, passageways, and dead end trails.

Early Spanish explorers charted this region, and often used the trails that wound through the lava beds on their journeys from the rich gold and silver mines in Colorado to Mexico City. They learned of the intricate and complicated passes through the rugged, black lava beds from the local Indians. The Spanish referred to this region as the malpais – bad country.

Sometime during the year 1770, a pack train moved slowly and single file along one of the routes winding through the malpais. The Spanish officer in charge of the train warily scanned the ridges as well as the trail ahead and behind. This was his third trip. He had never encountered so much as a single hostile Indian on previous journeys, but on entering this region days earlier he was warned repeatedly of increased depredations by the local tribes. In addition to his soldiers, all armed and excellent horsemen, the train consisted of fourteen pack mules, each one loaded with over 300 pounds of silver ingots.

The dry dust of the trail rose in swirls and eddies with the passage of the animals, and the only sound that could be heard was the clopping of hooves and an occasional curse from one of the men.

The officer was concerned. Deep in the marrow of his bones he was convinced something bad was going to occur before the day was over. He cautioned his soldiers to be extra vigilant as they wound their way through the twisting basaltic maze. The Spaniards had been on the trail for nearly one month, having left the mines near what is now Durango, Colorado, with as much silver as they were able to transport.

The officer became even more concerned as the pack train entered a region in the lava beds called The Narrows. The passageway was just over 100 yards long and so tight that a rider could reach out with both arms and touch the adjacent walls. It would be a perfect place for an ambush, thought the officer.

Unknown to the Spaniards, as the last rider passed through the entrance to The Narrows, approximately two dozen Indians rose up from their hiding places among the basalt and entered the passageway, effectively closing it to any retreat.

At the opposite end of The Narrows, the trail opened into a wide, grassy meadow where the officer intended to allow the men to rest and the animals to graze. Beyond the meadow was another long, narrow passageway that eventually opened out onto the plains to the south.

On arriving at the meadow, the officer ordered a temporary halt and instructed his men to unsadlle and unpack the animals and turn them loose to graze. Saddles, gear, provisions, and the packs containing the silver ingots were all stacked in the shade of an overhanging rock.

As the soldiers reclined in the coolness of the shade and sipped from their canteens, several Indians appeared at the opening of the passageway. The officer saw them first and alerted his men. Almost instantly, the Spaniards retrieved their arms and stood at the ready.

For nearly an hour the two opposing forces regarded each other, each assessing the strength of the other. Suddenly, at a cry from their leader, the Indians commenced shooting arrows into the midst of the soldiers, wounding two. In response, the Spaniards raised and fired their heavy muskets at the Indians. By the time the smoke had cleared, at least a half-dozen were down, dead or wounded. After retrieving their fallen comrades, the Indians quickly retreated back into the passageway.

As the officer discussed the options of fighting or fleeing with his soldiers, more Indians appeared on the rim above the meadow and fired arrows and hurled spears at the Spaniards, forcing them to retreat underneath the rock overhang. The men were safe from attack from above but were unable to return fire.

Here, the Spaniards took shelter for several days. Now and then one would venture out to attempt a shot at the Indians, but was invariably struck by arrows.

After the fifth day of hiding under the overhang, the officer noted the party was getting low on provisions. Since it was impossible to engage the enemy in battle as a result of their own inferior position, he decided they should effect a hasty escape through the southern passageway. Since the heavily laden mules would inhibit their flight, the officer ordered all of the silver buried beneath the overhang. A long, narrow trench was excavated and thousands of pounds of ingots were placed within and covered. The officer walked to the nearest wall of the shelter and carved the image of a coiled snake into the dark basalt to mark the location. A serpent was a traditional Spanish symbol often used to indicate the proximity of a significant treasure.

When all of the soldiers were packed and ready, the officer signaled it was time for the escape. Unable to retrieve and saddle their horses without making themselves easy targets, the Spaniards ran as fast as they could go from the overhang to the entrance to the southern passageway. During the flight, several of the Spaniards were struck and killed by arrows. Those who managed to reach the passageway were immediately slaughtered by a contingent of Indians who awaited them there. Within minutes, every Spaniard was scalped, mutilated, and dismembered.

The Indians then stormed into the grassy meadow and, after securing all of the Spaniards' horses and mules, rode away. They either did not notice or express any concern about the long trench that had been dug up and then covered over under the rock overhang.

With the passage of many years, the remains of the Spaniards rotted away and their bones gnawed and scattered by rodents and coyotes. Here and there along the narrow trail and in the grassy meadow, pieces of Spanish armor and fittings lay on the ground rusting.

Nearly one hundred years later, settlers began moving into this region, settlers who brought with them great herds of cattle and a desire to carve out a living in this rough and forbidding landscape. Cattle and horses were occasionally grazed in the few open meadows found within the lava beds, and once in a while a newcomer would find a rusted piece of Spanish armor, a spur, or a metal bridle or saddle fitting. None of the newcomers were aware of the incredible fortune in silver ingots buried beneath the rock overhang somewhere near the center of these extensive lava beds.

One of the newcomers to this region was a cattleman named Solomon Bilbo. Bilbo's wife was a member of a local Indian tribe, and from her people he often heard the handed-down story of the massacre of the Spaniards who, according to the tale, may have been transporting a treasure in silver from the rich mines in Colorado. Intrigued, Bilbo spent much of his free time searching throughout the malpais for the treasure. He found a number of locations that matched the description provided in the Indian legend, but he never located any buried silver.

In 1934, a young Indian approximately twenty-four years of age arrived at the York Ranch near Gallup. Though he never revealed where he obtained it, he carried a very old map that purported to show the location of a large buried treasure consisting of hundreds of silver ingots, a location purported to be near the center of the malpais. Years later, it was learned that this map had been taken from the body of the slain Spanish officer following the slaughter, a map which remained in the possession of the man's tribe for over 150 years.

Those who saw the map claimed that the location of the treasure was marked by the image of a coiled serpent.

With the aid of several cowhands, the Indian conducted a search of the grassy meadows known to be located within the confines of the lava beds but, again, no treasure was ever found. The Indian eventually left the area and was never seen again.

During the early 1950s, a young cowhand in the employ of the York Ranch rode into headquarters seeking treatment for a rattlesnake bite. While he was being doctored, the foreman asked where the incident occurred and the cowhand told him it happened while he was taking some shade under a rock overhand near one of the grassy meadows. On the back wall of the rock shelter, stated the cowboy, was an image of a coiled snake scratched into the stone.

The story was related to the owner of the ranch who happened to be familiar with the old Indian legend of the lost Spanish treasure. The following morning, the owner and foreman rode out to a grassy meadow they believed to be the one where the young man was bitten by the snake. They rode around the perimeter, spotted several rock overhangs, but never found the image of the serpent scratched into the rock. Later when they returned to the ranch, they sought out the youth to obtain more specific directions just to learn the cowboy had died from the snakebite only hours earlier.

*   *   *

The search for the lost lava beds treasure continues. A number of well-supplied expeditions have entered the malpais in recent years to try to locate the huge cache, but to date it remains hidden.

BLACK JACK CHRISTIAN'S
LOST TRAIN ROBBERY CACHE

Just as the sun was going down on the evening of November 6, 1897, Black Jack Christian emerged from behind a water tower in Grants, New Mexico, approached the recently arrived train with drawn revolver and pointed it at the fireman, Henry Abel. Abel had just jumped from the engine of the Santa Fe train onto the loading dock and was about conduct an inspection when confronted by the armed intruder. Christian immediately ordered Abel back into the engine, and as the two climbed aboard, the sound of gunfire erupted from the passenger coaches. Abel's worst fears were being realized—the train was being robbed.

As two masked outlaws went from passenger to passenger relieving them of their money and jewelry, Christian ordered Abel to pull the train approximately one mile farther up the track. A few minutes later as the gas lights of Grants slowly faded in the distance, the baggage, mail, and express cars were detached as the engine and the passenger cars proceeded down the track another two miles.

When the train stopped, Christian prompted Abel along at gunpoint until the two men came to the express car. Here they were joined by the other two outlaws, one of whom attached a dynamite charge to the heavy sliding door. Only seconds after the four men took cover behind a nearby cottonwood tree, an explosion blew apart the entire side of the express car. As Christian stood guard over Abel, his two companions entered the demolished car and located the heavy steel Wells-Fargo safe. Another charge was attached to the safe, this one removing the door and exposing the contents within. In moments, the outlaws had scooped over one hundred thousand dollars in gold and silver coins out of the destroyed safe and into saddlebags which were, in turn, loaded onto spare horses.

Bidding fireman Abel a polite "good night", Black Jack Christian and his two companions rode away into the darkness wealthier men.

Abel made a mental note of the direction of the escape route and then promptly returned the train to the depot at Grants. After wiring railroad and law enforcement authorities of the robbery, Abel was joined the following afternoon by a contingent of Wells-Fargo agents, railroad detectives, the Cibola County sheriff, and several men recently deputized specifically for the anticipated pursuit. Abel explained to all that Christian and his two companions rode toward the lava beds located south of Grants. This rugged landscape, composed of ancient and weathered basalt from eons-old volcanic eruptions, was a temporary home to hostile Indians as well as outlaws. Twisting and sometimes dead-end trails wound through the lava beds, and on more than one occasion travelers who entered this forbidding region were never seen again.

The posse, composed of some fifteen men, pursued the bandits for three days before giving up and returning to Grants. Once in the lava beds, the pursuers lost the trail of the train robbers. At one point during the chase, it was learned later, the posse had passed within one hundred yards of the outlaws' camp without realizing it.

The day after the search party returned to Grants, a large reward was offered for Black Jack Christian, dead or alive, but the trail of the outlaws had grown cold.

Following their escape after the robbery and a long night of hard riding into the lava beds, Christian and his two henchmen stopped at an old Indian campsite deep within the confines of the black, rugged malpais. The site offered a fresh water spring and adequate protection from the unceasing and harsh desert winds. More importantly, it afforded an excellent defensive position should pursuing lawmen track them to this location.

During the early morning hours and after a meal of bacon was cooked on the low campfire, the three outlaws opened a bottle of whiskey to celebrate their successful robbery. For the next two hours and as the morning sun rose, the men became drunk and fell to arguing among themselves relative to the division of the gold and silver coins.

One of Christian's henchmen, suddenly angered by a comment from the other, yanked his revolver from the holster and shot the antagonist through the head, killing him instantly. Several hours later as Christian and the murderer were excavating a hole in which they intended to bury the dead bandit, they heard the sounds of men and horses riding along a nearby trail—It was the posse that had earlier ridden out of Grants. Christian climbed to an elevated knob and spotted the riders not more than one hundred yards away. Scurrying back to the campsite, Christian informed the other of the proximity of the lawmen and the need for escape. In order to affect an unimpeded flight, the two men tossed the heavy coin-filled saddlebags into the newly excavated hole. Atop these they laid the body of the dead outlaw. After refilling the hole, the two mounted their horses and rode southward and out of the lava beds.

The following day, Christian suggested the two split up to confuse any pursuing lawmen. They agreed to meet in thirty days at Silver City. From there, he instructed, they would return to the lava beds and retrieve the treasure.

Two weeks later, however, Black Jack Christian was wounded while attempting another train robbery a short distance from Silver City. A few days later, his companion was subdued and arrested during an attempted train robbery in eastern Arizona. He was sentenced to twenty years in the Yuma Territorial Prison but died from consumption after serving only five.

Christian lived for two days following his aborted train robbery attempt. Before he died, he told the Catron County sheriff about robbing the Santa Fe train at Grants and burying the gold and silver coins at his hideout in the lava beds. Encouraged by the sheriff, Christian related directions to the site. The sheriff subsequently led two expeditions into the lava beds in search of the cache but, once there, found Christian's directions and estimated distances vague and confusing. Frustrated, he finally gave up.

During the summer of 1894, an out-of-work cowboy traveling through the lava beds made camp one evening in the shelter of a small, secluded grassy area well within the malpais. After filling his canteen from the small spring and bringing coffee to boil over his campfire, he noticed a small mound of dirt several feet from where he squatted. Curious, he dug into the mound only to encounter a skeleton and some rotted clothing. Spooked by the discovery, he quickly refilled the hole and returned to his coffee.

Had the cowboy removed the skeleton and dug another inch or two beyond, he would have discovered a fortune well beyond his wildest dreams.

Years later when the cowboy was an old man with grandchildren, he was told the story of the Grants train robbery and Black Jack Christian's death bed tale of the location of the buried loot. The old cowboy realized he had found the location of the treasure decades earlier without knowing it.

Over the course of the next two years, the old cowboy undertook several trips into the rugged lava beds in an attempt to relocate that same campsite, the one with the fresh water spring, the one that offered sanctuary from the dessicating desert winds.

He never found it. The great fortune in gold and silver coins lies there today just beneath the skeleton of a long-dead train robber, an estimated one million dollars worth of century-old loot in today's values awaiting the patient searcher or simply a lucky passer-by.

THE CURSE OF THE LOST ADAMS DIGGINGS

Throughout the history and geography of New Mexico, few tales of lost mines and buried treasures are more familiar to professional and amateur treasure hunters alike than that of the Lost Adams Diggings, believed by many researchers to lie somewhere in the west-central part of the state not far from the Arizona border. Here, a small, ephemeral stream runs through a narrow, zig-zag canyon, once the home to warring Apaches led by the feared warrior Chief Nana. In the bottom of this stream and mixed with the sands and gravels eroded and transported from the nearby mountains can be found an incredibly rich deposit of placer gold.

Well over a century ago this gold was discovered and harvested by men who died because of it. Following the subsequent abandonment of the site and the related mining activity, its exact location has been lost. Men have searched, and continue to search, for the uncountable wealth that awaits in this mysterious and remote canyon.

* * *

The man known only as Adams, the figure whose name is associated with what many consider to be the richest gold placer mine in America, remains an enigmatic figure.

He once admitted to having been born in Rochester, New York on 10 July 1829 but revealed little else of his background. Even his first name has been lost in the maze and mire of the history of the American Southwest.

It is known, however, that Adams drove a freight wagon and delivered goods from Los Angeles, California, to Tucson, Arizona, and back. By all accounts, he was a competent and loyal employee of the freight company and appeared content with his job.

Sometime during August of 1864, Adams had delivered a load of freight in Tucson, collected a $2,000 payment, and was on the road back to California driving a freshly loaded wagon and trailer and leading a string of twelve horses. A few days later he set up a night camp just off the road near Gila Bend. As was his custom when transporting horses, Adams turned the animals loose to graze on the lush grasses that grew along the floodplain of the Gila River while he slept.

Just before dawn, Adams was stirred awake by the sound of hoof beats. Rising from his bedroll, he spotted a half-dozen Apache youths running off his horses. After buckling on his gunbelt and grabbing his rifle, Adams pursued the horse thieves on foot, eventually encountering them an hour later where they halted in a shallow arroyo some two miles away. The Apaches were unaware of Adam's arrival, and while they were distracted with their newly acquired herd of horses, the freighter crept closer. Taking them completely by surprise, Adams fired his rifle into their midst, killing two of them and driving away the others.

After gathering the horses, Adams herded them back to the campsite only to discover his wagon and trailer afire and his harnesses and other tack cut to pieces. Apparently, the stealing of the horses was a diversion so that his camp could be looted.

With the dozen horses in tow, Adams rode several miles to a Pima Indian village he had passed the previous day. There, he intended to trade a few of the animals for enough supplies to get him back to California.

Just before reaching the village, Adams encountered a group of some twenty miners who were panning for gold in a nearby stream. The miners told Adams they were on their way to some promising gold fields in California and were hoping to retrieve enough placer gold at this site to fund the remainder of their journey. Several of the miners were interested in Adams' horses and commenced bartering with him. As Adams visited with the miners, a young Mexican dressed in the garb of an Apache joined them and watched the proceedings.

For the rest of the day, the Mexican followed Adams around the camp of the miners and later in the Pima village. During an evening meal, the young man told Adams that he and a brother were stolen from their families deep in Mexico by Apaches and carried north into Arizona. His brother was eventually killed by a member of the tribe, and after several years the Apaches finally abandoned him near this very same Pima village where he was taken in and treated well.

On the right side of his head, the Mexican sported a deformed ear that resembled a knotted piece of rope. He was given the name Gotch Ear by the Pimas.

Each time one of the miners retrieved a tiny amount of gold flake from the bottom of the little stream they worked, Gotch Ear reacted with amusement. When Adams asked him why, the Mexican replied that he knew of a canyon, a two-week ride to the northeast, where so much gold could be gathered in a single day that a stout mule would not be able to carry it all. Gotch Ear claimed that while living with the Apaches, he had seen with his own eyes nuggets as large as wild grapes lying at the bottom of the narrow stream that flowed through the remote canyon.

Later, Adams repeated Gotch Ear's story to the miners, all of whom became excited about the possibilities of finding great wealth in the far away location. The miners asked Adams if he would negotiate with the Mexican to lead them to the gold. Following a brief parley, Gotch Ear agreed to lead Adams and the miners to the canyon in exchange for one of the horses, a saddle, a rifle, and some ammunition.

On the morning of August 20, 1864, Adams and the miners, led by Gotch Ear, rode and walked out of the Pima village on their way to the canyon of gold. During the long journey, Adams attempted to take note of landmarks along the way. Adams, unfortunately, had a poor sense of direction and detail and was unable to remember much of the country he passed through. His inability to recall such important elements was to plague him for remainder of his life.

Days later, the party crossed the pass between what were later identified as Mounts Ord and Thomas in eastern Arizona. Years later, Adams related that during this trip the group had also passed by the White Mountains and crossed two large rivers, most likely the Black and the Little Colorado. Following this they crossed a well-traveled wagon road that Gotch Ear claimed led to Fort Wingate some distance to the north.

One evening after two weeks of traveling, Gotch Ear led the party to a suitable campsite a short distance from a fresh water spring. The following morning, the Mexican told Adams that they were now close to the canyon of gold and warned him that this was the territory of feared Apache Chief Nana. The Apaches, he claimed, often camped in the canyon they were about to enter. Nana and his warriors had often slain white miners and travelers who passed through his homeland. Adams and the miners grew uneasy at this information.

As the miners ate breakfast, Adams noted that not far from the campsite was an irrigated and cultivated pumpkin patch. Gotch Ear explained that the Apache women tended to the planting and harvesting of the pumpkins as well as corn and squash.

After repacking supplies onto the horses, the miners followed Gotch Ear into the entrance of a canyon located just to the northeast. The trip through the canyon was slow and difficult owing to the rough and rocky bottom. Presently, Gotch Ear arrived at a narrow opening along one wall of the canyon, a passageway partially hidden by a large boulder. Following the Mexican through the cumbersome opening, the miners proceeded down a gently sloping trail littered with boulders large and small, all making travel difficult. Segments of this second canyon were so narrow that a man could touch both walls with his hands as he walked or rode though it. Adams later described the route through the canyon as Z-shaped.

An hour or so later, the narrow canyon widened somewhat into a small valley filled with pine trees and through which a narrow stream trickled. At the northwestern end of the little valley and around a bend was a waterfall approximately eight to ten feet high. Beyond the far ridge, two rounded mountain tops protruded—Gotch Ear identified them as the Peloncillo Mountains.

As Adams and the miners regarded the little valley they just entered, Gotch Ear pointed to the narrow, shallow, slow-moving creek and told them that is where they will find the gold. Though exhausted from the difficult travel through the rugged canyons, the miners secured their gold pans and made their way to the stream. Minutes later, excited shouts from the miners echoed off adjacent granite walls as they harvested gold nuggets aplenty from the waters.

Two days later Gotch Ear informed Adams he was ready to leave. After he was presented with a fine horse and saddle, a rifle, and some ammunition, Adams and the miners bade him a good journey. The Mexican waved as he rode away. Gotch Ear was never seen again. Months later Adams learned that one of Nana's warriors was seen riding the horse that was given to the Mexican.

During the next few days as more and more gold was accumulated, Adams fell into the role as leader of the group. At his suggestion, the miners agreed to collect all of their gold, store it in a common location, and divide it equally at a later date.

When not panning gold from the stream, several of the miners busied themselves with the construction of a log cabin to shelter them against the coming winter. At one end of the cabin, as per Adams' instructions, a large, rock hearth was constructed. Beneath the hearth, a chamber was excavated, one lined with flat stones and into which was placed the growing accumulation of gold.

At one point during the construction of the cabin, the miners were visited by Chief Nana and a group of some two dozen armed and mounted warriors. Addressing Adams, Nana demanded an explanation as to why his valley was filled with white men. Adams told the Apache that they only wished to pan for gold and represented no threat to the Indians whatsoever. Nana acknowledged that the gold was of little use to the Apache and he agreed to allow the men to remain if they promised to respect the valley and the water. He cautioned them not to overhunt wild game. Growing stern, Nana voiced a harsh warning against trespassing into the upper part of the little valley he which he called Sno-ta-hay canyon. The area was considered sacred, he said, and if any violated the agreement, death would visit the miners one and all.

Weeks passed and provisions grew low. Adams elected to send a party of eight men to Fort Wingate for food, ammunition, and other supplies. A miner named John Brewer was placed in charge of the small expedition. Brewer estimated it would take approximately eight days to make the trip.

While awaiting the return of their companions and the provisions, the miners continued to take gold from the little stream, each one amazed that there appeared to be no end to the wealth thay lay there in the sands. By this time, Adams estimated just over $100,000 worth of nuggets had been collected and placed in the secret chamber beneath the hearth.

Each day, the miners spotted members of Nana's tribe observing them from nearby ridges.

Four days after Brewer and his party left for Fort Wingate, one of the miners showed Adams a gold nugget the leader later described as being "as large as a hen's egg." When Adams asked where it was found, the miner replied he pulled several of them from the stream bottom just above the waterfall. Adams reminded him and the other miners of the warning given by Nana and cautioned them to refrain from entering the sacred ground of the Apache.

Unknown to Adams, five of the miners, lured by the promise of the large gold nuggets, snuck away from camp that night and panned gold from the stream beyond the waterfall. The next morning, one of the miners showed Adams a coffeepot filled with the huge nuggets. Again, Adams repeated Nana's warning, but the remaining miners, after gazing upon the large nuggets, scrambled upstream to retrieve more of the same.

On the evening of the eighth day following Brewer's departure, Adams began to grow worried. When the group failed to appear the following morning, Adams, along with a miner named Davidson, rode into the zig-zag canyon in hopes of meeting their companions. Adams confessed to harboring a sinking feeling in his stomach during the ride.

By the time the two men had reached the narrow, hidden opening to the larger canyon their worst fears were realized. Lying scattered upon the ground were the dead, scalped, and mutilated bodies of five of their fellows. Littering the rocky ground between the bodies were remnants of the recently purchased supplies. On reaching this point during their return from Fort Wingate, Adams deduced, the group was attacked and slaughtered by the Apaches. Adams fervently hoped the other three miners had escaped.

Worried that their friends back at the camp might be in danger, Adams and Davidson hurried back down the zig-zag canyon to warn of potential attack. On reaching the end of the canyon, however, they heard gunshots, the hoarse shouts of the miners, and the shrill screams of the Apaches. Gazing in horror at what met their eyes, Adams and Davidson watched as three hundred mounted Indians rode up and down this part of the valley attacking and killing the miners one by one. As the dead men were scalped and hacked to pieces, the cabin was set afire.

Fearing discovery, Adams and Davidson quickly dismounted and crawled into a dense cover of brush. From their place of concealment, the two men watched as the Indians fought over scalps, the dead miners' clothes, and the division of the few remaining supplies. Just before sundown, the Indians rode away and out of sight beyond the waterfall.

When they were certain the Apaches were gone, Adams and Davidson cautiously crept down to the cabin with the intention of retrieving the gold hidden beneath the hearth. On arriving, however, the intense heat from the still-burning embers and logs prevented them from reaching the nuggets. Fearful the Apaches might return, the two men hurried back up the little valley and into the narrow canyon. The only gold carried from the valley was the large nugget earlier given to Adams and which he carried in a pocket.

Adams and Davidson found their horses farther up in the canyon, mounted up, and rode the rest of the way out. Without pausing, they spurred their mounts down the rough trail past the pumpkin patch in the hope of reaching safety.

Days later with no food to eat, Adams and Davidson killed one of their horses and dined on the blood and the meat of a haunch. Riding double on the remaining horse, they were discovered two weeks later by a platoon of U.S. Cavalry from Fort Apache. The two survivors were taken to the fort and admitted to the hospital where they were treated for malnutrition and exhaustion.

Davidson, who was in his fifties and of a weak constitution, eventually succumbed to the ordeal and died several days later.

Adams was never the same. While living at Fort Wingate during his recovery, he found a pistol and shot and killed two young Apaches who were serving as scouts. Adams claimed the two were among the raiders who slaughtered his friends. Adams was charged with murder, but while he languished in the Fort Wingtate jail awaiting trial, a sympathetic officer allowed him to escape. Fleeing west, Adams stopped in Tucson long enough to sell the gold nugget he still carried. From there, he proceeded to Los Angeles, California, where he was eventually reunited with his wife and three children.

For the next ten years, Adams suffered horrible night-mares in which he relived the ordeal of watching his friends attacked, killed, and mutilated by the Apaches in the canyon of gold. Though he knew that a vast fortune awaited him should he only return to the canyon and retrieve some of the ore, Adams could not bring himself to do it in fear of encountering Chief Nana and his blood-thirsty warriors.

*   *   *

A retired ship captain named C. A. Shaw heard of the story of the canyon of old and eventually located Adams in California. Intrigued by the possibilities of finding it, Shaw offered to finance an expedition into the area, agree-ing to pay Adams handsomely to serve as guide. Adams, now forty-five years of age, demurred, but after consider-able coaxing by Shaw finally agreed to the proposition.

During the expedition, Adams became lost time and again and was unable to recognize any pertinent land-marks. During the next decade, Shaw undertook several more expeditions, each time involving Adams, but was never able to locate the lost canyon of gold.

The physician who treated Adams at Fort Wingate became keenly interested in the canyon of gold as a result of listening to his patient's provocative tale. Using details and directions provided by Adams, the doctor, hardly an outdoorsman, ventured out into the rugged mountain range. Unfortunately, he suffered from the rigors and hardships of the search and was never able to mount a sat-isfactory expedition. Though he searched for the canyon on several other occasions he never found it. The physician, in turn, told the story to a man named John Dowling.

Dowling had experience as a miner and a commercial hunter and was no stranger to the wilderness. He was also somewhat familiar with the mountain range in which he believed the mysterious canyon to be located, having successfully panned gold from many of the small streams found in its canyons. During his search, Dowling entered and rode through a narrow, zig-zag canyon which opened up into a small valley. Here, he related, he found over sixty tree stumps. He reasoned the trees had been cut down to provide logs for a cabin. A short distance farther up the valley Dowling came upon a very old pile of ash and charcoal next to what was once a rock hearth and chimney. At the time, Dowling did not know of the existence of the large cache of gold nuggets lying in the chamber beneath the hearth.

For several days, Dowling panned in the little stream and recovered small amounts of gold. He located the waterfall but never examined the stream bottom above it for signs of gold. Ultimately discouraged, however, he left the canyon never to return.

While traveling through New Mexico one year, Adams met a man named Bob Lewis in the town of Magdelena. Lewis told Adams he had searched for the lost placer mine for years but with no success. Using additional information he gleaned from his conversation with Adams, Lewis set out on another expedition in the Datil Mountains in search of the canyon and, he claimed, found it.

With luck, Lewis located and rode through the partially hidden entrance to the narrow, zig-zag canyon. On entering the canyon, he discovered the skeletal remains of several men and a number of horses. These, he concluded, were what was left of the group of men sent to Fort Wingate for supplies.

Lewis entered the valley containing the little stream and remained there panning for gold for nearly a week. Like Dowling who came before him, Lewis inexplicably did not attempt to pan for gold above the waterfall where the egg-sized nuggets were found by members of Adam's party. Finding barely enough ore to fill only half of a small poke, Lewis finally gave up and returned to Magdalena.

Sometime during the summer of 1888, a man accompanied by his wife and daughter pulled up to the ranch house of John Tenney. The Tenney Ranch was located on the west flank of the Datil Mountains in Catron County. Behind the wagon was a herd of some twenty cattle and a few horses. After climbing down from the wagon, the man requested permission from Tenney to camp nearby on his ranch and graze his tired and hungry stock for a day or two. Tenney readily agreed and pointed to a good location about a hundred yards away.

Later that evening, Tenney walked over to the campsite to visit with the travelers. The newcomer introduced himself as John Brewer. Tenney, who knew the story of what had come to be called the Lost Adams Diggings, asked if he was the same John Brewer who had accompanied Adams to the fateful canyon of gold. The newcomer admitted he was.

For the next two hours, Brewer related to Tenney his version of the events of that time some twenty-four years earlier. Though badly wounded, Brewer and two of his companions managed to escape from the Apaches at the mouth of the narrow canyon and fled westward into the desert. Days later he was found by friendly Indians and taken to their village. It took almost three months for him to recover from his ordeal. He never learned what happened to his two friends.

Though often tempted to return to the canyon for the gold cache, Brewer could never bring himself to do so, believing the area was cursed. Looking Tenney in the eye,

Brewer told him there was more gold in that canyon than ten kings could spend in a lifetime.

*   *   *

The Lost Adams Diggings has been the object of hundreds of searches, but those who look for it come away perplexed at their inability to locate it. More than a dozen different locations have been identified as a possible site.

In recent years an amazing discovery was made by a Colorado resident. Employing information he acquired, he traveled to a location near the Arizona-New Mexico border and entered a canyon he is convinced was the same one to which Adams and the twenty miners were led by the Mexican guide, Gotch Ear. The canyon has a pronounced zig-zag shape and near the end is an old line shack once used by cowboys. Closer inspection, however, reveals abundant evidence of a long ago fire, one that left deposits of ash and charred timbers beneath the shack. Nearby is a very old, tumbled down rock hearth, next to which was found a hidden chamber. The chamber was empty.

Several yards upstream can be found a waterfall, and just beyond lies a site entirely suitable as a campground, quite possibly the one Chief Nana claimed as his own.

Everything about the canyon suggests it could be the location of the Lost Adams Diggings. All that is needed to solidify the evidence is to find gold in the little, narrow stream that courses through the area.

The finder was not equipped to pan for gold at the time of his discovery. On returning to his home in Colorado, however, he was stricken with a heart attack which left him in poor health and unable to return.

Was he yet another victim of what Brewer referred to as the curse of the Lost Adams Diggings? Many believe he was.

The Lost Gold
of Alamocita Creek

One of the earliest roads in the western United States that saw siginificant commercial use was one that ran from Fort Whipple, Arizona (near present-day Prescott), eastward into New Mexico before bearing northeastward toward Denver.

This same road was originally used with some regularity by the Spaniards during the sixteenth century while exploring and settling this area. They subsequently followed the road when hauling freight and transporting colonists. During the nineteenth century, a number of wagon trains traveled this road, carrying eager settlers westward. Later, as mines and mineral processing developed in Arizona, products of gold and silver were transported along the same route on their way to the Denver Mint.

To travel this road today is to wonder why such a route was ever used. The terrain is extremely rugged and boulder-strewn, the passes are often steep and difficult to traverse even with modern vehicles, and, except for two isolated locations, very little water can be found along most of its length. During the 1800s, the region of New Mexico through which the road passed was homeland to warring Apaches who often resented trespass by others.

Sometime during the late 1860s, two stout, heavily-laden wagons left Fort Whipple. The wagons, drawn by oxen, were loaded with heavy ingots of gold from nearby mines and bound for the United States Mint at Denver. Each wagon was handled by a pair of skilled Mexican drivers, and only two mounted guards accompanied the small train. The prevailing thinking of the day was that a large contingent guards only attracted attention to the cargo being transported, so freight companies often tried to appear inconspicuous by sending along only a small party of armed riders.

Though travel was slow and tiresome, the wagon train moved consistently along the old road until reaching Alamocita Creek, a tributary of the Rio Salado in western Socorro County. Though narrow and often ephemeral, Alamocita Creek was generally anticipated by travelers through the region. Along its banks were numerous campsites where travelers and freighters rested the stock and themselves before continuing on their journey. A few miles downstream where the creek joined the Rio Salado, the trail turned toward the northeast and became somewhat less rugged and difficult to travel.

It was early one morning as the drivers and guards were preparing breakfast at an Alamocita campsite when the Apaches attacked without warning. Within minutes, every member of the wagon train party was killed, scalped, and hacked to pieces. While several of the Indians cut the oxen loose and drove them away, the remainder rifled through the backs of the wagons in search of something salvageable. Before long, the braves were squabbling over the few changes of clothes carried by the drivers and guards.

On finding the gold, the Apaches grew concerned. They were well aware of the white man's lust for this precious metal, and the Indians' encounters with prospectors and miners in this and neighboring ranges were many. Fearing that others who knew about the gold shipment would come in search of it and possibly bring the United States Army, the Indians decided to hide it. After unloading the ingots from the wagon, they carried them to a nearby cave and dumped them within.

Days passed, and when the shipment of gold did not arrive at the Denver mint on schedule, a telegraph was sent to Fort Whipple. A platoon of cavalry was subsequently assigned to follow the road and try to determine what became of the gold shipment and the drivers.

After many days of hard travel, the cavalry contingent came upon the scene of the bloody massacre approximately midway along the length of Alamocita Creek. The badly decomposed remains of the mutilated men were buried in two separate graves. Atop the graves were placed charred remains of the wagons—wheel rims, bolts, metal bridle fittings, and trace chains.

Though the cavalrymen searched a wide area in hope of finding the gold, they were unsuccessful. Finally, they returned to Fort Whipple.

*   *   *

As settlers moved into the western part of Socorro County and established ranches along Alamocita Creek and Rio Salado, the story of the wagon train massacre and the lost gold shipment was related time and again. Several of the newcomers attempted to find the gold but the demands of raising cattle and sheep in this rough country took up most of their time. Presently, the tale became part and parcel of the local lore. Organized searches for the gold subsided and, with time, eventually ceased altogether.

*   *   *

In 1889, an elderly Apache living in Magdalena, some forty miles southeast of Alamocita Creek, was interviewed by a young woman who was writing a book on the region. She asked the old man several questions about the relations between the Apaches and the early settlers in the area, but she got more than she bargained for.

During the course of the interview, the Indian admitted he was a member of the war party that attacked the wagon train near Alamocita Creek and was among those who killed the drivers and guards. He was, he stated, one of several who unloaded the heavy gold ingots from the wagon beds and threw them into a nearby cave. This done, he said, the cave was filled in with rock and dirt and made to look like the rest of the environment.

Several weeks passed, and the young woman related the story of the old Indian's part in the wagon train massacre to several people. A rancher named McCord, accompanied by a neighbor, traveled to Magdalena to talk with the old man to try to gain some insight into the location of the gold ingot-filled cave. McCord had searched for the gold many times and was convinced it was hidden not far from the site of the massacre.

As with the young woman, the Apache provided details of the attack, the burning of the wagons, and the hiding of the gold. When McCord asked for specific directions to the cave, the Indian replied that he was unable to provide directions, but that if he could go to the site he would be able to point to the hidden cave. It was not very far from the place where the wagoneers stopped to camp, he said.

As preparations were being made to carry the old man to Alamocita Creek, he died. With his death went the knowledge of the exact location of the lost wagon train gold.

*   *   *

Visitors to the Alamocita Creek massacre site today can still see the two graves in which the slain drivers and guards were interred, the metal wagon and harness fittings placed atop them over a century ago scattered about by animals and time. Not far from these graves at some unknown location lies a hidden cave containing an incredible fortune in gold ingots.

WICKS GULCH GOLD

For over a century, Wicks Gulch in Sierra County has been a well-known and favored location among placer gold miners. This site, some three miles east of the town of Hillsboro, has yielded significant amounts of gold over the years, and men have grown moderately wealthy from panning the flakes and nuggets found there. Today, eager placer miners continue to visit Wicks Gulch to harvest the gold from the ephemeral stream bottom.

An additional incentive for coming to Wicks Gulch is a buried treasure. Somewhere a short distance from the paved highway that crosses the gulch is buried an old cast-iron cooking pot in which some 2,500 ounces of raw gold were hidden during the 1880s.

* * *

The man credited for first discovering gold in Wicks Gulch was George Wells. Wells had prospected the rock outcrops in Sierra County and the surrounding region for many years before striking it rich. In just a few months time during the winter of 1877-1878, Wells panned close to $100,000 worth of gold from Wicks Gulch, an amount considered to be an impressive fortune during this time. Wells quit his mining operation a short time later and moved to

El Paso, Texas, where he invested heavily in real estate and became even wealthier.

In 1882, two mining partners—Jim Bradley and Henry Whitehead—filed a pair of claims in Wicks Gulch. Whitehead's part of the claim included the location from which Wells had taken most of his placer gold. Whitehead found this site still very rich in the metal, and in a short time had accumulated close to 2,500 ounces of gold. Rather than carry his gold to Hillsboro and exchange it for cash, Whitehead preferred to keep it in an old cast-iron cookpot. When the pot was nearly full, Whitehead buried it a short distance from the crude rock cabin in which he lived, a cabin originally constructed by Wells a few years earlier.

Whitehead's nephew, a young man named Gordon Bourke-Wilder, occasionally accompanied his uncle out to Wicks Gulch and helped him pan for gold. Though impressed with his uncle's fortune, Bourke-Wilder was not particularly interested in mining and found greater satisfaction working as a cowhand on area ranches.

During the summer of 1882, Bourke-Wilder told his uncle that he had accepted a job as foreman on a large ranch in Mexico but needed to borrow some money to purchase a new horse, saddle, and other tack. Whitehead readily agreed to lend his nephew the money. After instructing the young man to wait in the cabin, Whitehead walked outside and was gone for approximately fifteen minutes. When he returned, he handed Bourke-Wilder a pouch of gold that was sufficient to cover his needed purchases. At the time, he explained to his nephew that his gold had been placed in an old cooking pot and was buried nearby.

The following December, Bourke-Wilder returned to Sierra County from Mexico to spend the holidays with relatives. One morning he rode out to Wicks Gulch to visit his uncle and to pay him back the money he owed. Unable to find his uncle, Bourke-Wilder made inquiries from area residents and discovered his uncle was dead, having been murdered by robbers. In searching for his cached gold, the robbers tore apart the cabin but found nothing. They did, however, steal a shotgun belonging to Whitehead.

The Sierra County sheriff was notified of the murder. He quickly deputized three men and followed the trail of the killers. Two weeks later, two men were arrested far to the north in San Juan County. One of them was in the possession of Whitehead's shotgun, but neither of them carried any gold. During their subsequent trial, the two admitted killing the miner and looking for the cache of gold they knew he had hidden somewhere, but they never found it. The two were found guilty and hanged a few weeks later.

Bourke-Wilder returned to Wicks Gulch to try to find his uncle's cooking pot cache of placer gold. Though he dug in every probable location around the cabin he was never able to locate it. Bourke-Wilder searched for many weeks, but was finally forced to find work to return to his job as ranch foreman in order to earn a living.

*   *   *

Forty years later, Bourke-Wilder returned to Wicks Gulch to resume his search for his late uncle's 2,500 ounces of gold. He filed a number of claims in the region and even panned a significant amount of gold from the old Wells placer. Eventually, he moved into his uncle's old cabin and for the next several years he panned for gold along the length of Wicks Gulch and other nearby locations.

One day during the mid-1920s, Bourke-Wilder was found dead in his uncle's cabin. Though he searched for the buried pot of placer gold for most of his life, he never found it.

*   *   *

Unlike a lot of lost treasure locations, Wicks Gulch is far from being remote. In fact, a paved highway crosses the gulch just a few hundred feet from the ruins of the old Whitehead cabin.

Placer miners still occasionally come to this site, and sometimes a few days of panning yields a tiny pouch of gold. Though many know of the existence of placer gold to be found in Wicks Gulch, few are aware of the story of the lost gold cache of Henry Whitehead, one that contains 2,500 ounces of gold and is estimated to be worth over three-quarters of a million dollars today.

LOST FORTUNE IN SILVER IN TRES HERMANAS MOUNTAINS

During the early part of the twentieth century, a number of historical documents were discovered in the archives of an old monastery in Mexico City. Many of the documents, several of them almost 400 years old, related to the history of the establishment of the Catholic church in the lands claimed by Spain during the sixteenth and seventeenth centuries. A number of the documents also dealt with relations between the Spanish and the Indian tribes in the region, the founding of settlements and towns, and activities related to business pursuits such as trade, trapping, and mining.

It was during the examination of these documents by scholars from the United States and Europe that several describing locations of rich gold and silver mines were discovered. In addition, seven of the scrolls contained descriptions of several locations where gold and silver ingots as well as coins had been buried by the Spaniards.

One particularly tantalizing document involves an alleged huge treasure trove of silver coins along with an almost unbelieveable cache of ninety mule loads of silver ingots in the Tres Hermanas Mountains in Luna County of southwestern New Mexico.

In part, the document in question, translated from the Spanish, states:

Go to El Paso del Norte and find out where the Florida Mountains and the three hills called the Tres Hermanas Mountains are. Between the Florida Mountains and the Tres Hermanas Mountains is an old road leading from El Paso del Norte. Through the gaps of said mountains you strike a large plain which is very sandy until you reach Zapello Pass.

When you go through this pass you will cross another plain, leaving the mountain to your left. When you meet with some large, deep breaks you go through them and you shall meet with yet another very sandy plain. Upon reaching this plain the first thing you see is the Rallada Mountains to your left.

Look for the old main road and follow it until you reach the Potrillo Mountains. You will leave these mountains to your right as you follow the main road. Eventually you will arrive at a very large lake or lagoon. Leave this lake to your left and continue to follow the main road. Very shortly you will get to the heart of the Florida Mountains and the Tres Hermanas hills. On the first of three hills that you meet going that way you shall find a spring a short distance east of said hills and in the direction where the sun rises. About sixty yards from the spring you will find a stone with a badly cut cross made by the point of an iron bar. Move the stone and dig about ten feet. You will find forty mule loads of silver coins.

Now, go toward your left along the slope of the hill until you get to the middle of the pass formed by the two first hills. Here, you shall find a very rich mine called the San Miguel Mine. Ore from this mine was taken to the smelters in Ciudad Chihuahua. There is

a very large stone which covers the entrance to this
mine. The mine has four ladders inside. Just as soon
as you descend two ladders you will find bars of sil-
ver from ninety mules which we buried there.

Given directions as precise as those found in the document, one would assume it would be an easy thing to
locate this long lost buried treasure. In truth, following the
directions across this southwestern part of New Mexico
proved to be quite simple. Locating the actual silver coins
and ingots, however, was a different prospect. There is little doubt among researchers that these two large treasures are still hidden in the Tres Hermanas Mountains, but
the exact locations continue to elude searchers.

*   *   *

In 1968, a party of three professional treasure hunters
in possession of the above document left El Paso, Texas,
determined to follow the directions to the buried troves.
They found several roads that wound across the floor of
this portion of the Chihuahuan Desert, and selected the
one the believed was identified in the document.

From this trail, a number of "sandy plains" could be
observed prior to entering a pass. Though this pass is not
known today by the name Zapello Pass, it was clearly the
one mentioned in the writings. The "deep breaks" referred
to in the document were highly eroded arroyos, deep channels carved into the desert floor as a result of heavy runoff
from nearby mountains.

Another plain is crossed, with the Rallada Mountains
located just to the right of it. Continuing along on this
road, the members of the expedition came to the "lake"
referred to in the document. This topographic landform is
not a true lake, but is what is known as a playa. Playas are
shallow basins into which runoff flows and accumulates.

There is no drainage out of these playas, and the only way the water can leave is by seeping into the ground or by evaporation into the atmosphere. With hundreds, perhaps thousands of years of evaporation, most playas have thick deposits of salt in their beds. When dry, they are generally referred to by the locals as "salt flats." When they are filled with water resulting from the runoff of recent rains, they do appear to be lakes. It is likely that this one contained such runoff when first observed and described by the original writer of the document. There are, in fact, dozens of playas of various sizes throughout the region in question.

After continuing along the road, leaving the playa on the left, one passes between the Florida and Tres Hermanas mountain ranges with the route heading straight toward the Tres Hermanas.

On arriving at the first of the three peaks known as the Tres Hermanas (Three Sisters) Mountains, the men searched for a spring "a little bit east" of it. While no active spring was located, a number of sites were found that likely contained springs in years past. Subsequent investigation revealed that the pumping of the ground water for crop irrigation in this area has significantly lowered the water table which, in turn, resulted in the drying up of dozens of springs.

From each of the potential spring sites, the searchers ranged out looking for "a stone with a badly cut cross made by the point of an iron bar." Ten feet beneath this stone, according to the document, lies forty mules loads of silver coins.

Such a stone was never found. The searchers were convinced a stone like the one described did, in fact, exist, but concluded that the natural erosional and weathering processes associated with rain, freezing and thawing, and exfoliation erased all traces of the cross on the rock. As evidence for this, some of the carvings and scratches on nearby rocks made by miners in this area as recently as the 1930s were highly eroded and barely legible.

The three men hiked along the slope of the first peak to the middle of the pass between it and the second. Here, according to the document, was to be found the San Miguel Mine in which ninety mule loads of silver ingots were cached. There exist today several abandoned silver mines in this area, most of them dating back only to the 1930s. Whether or not one of the more recently operated mines was, in fact, the San Miguel Mine, is unknown. An examination of the records filed during the 1930s found no references to the discovery of ninety mules loads of silver.

Further studies of the old accounts stored in the Luna County courthouse did, however, reveal a curious discovery by an employee of one of the mining companies that held a mineral leases here fifty years earlier. The employee wrote that, during an afternoon off work from his labors in the mine, he was exploring around one side of the middle mountain of the Tres Hermanas range and discovered a small opening on the slope just above the pediment. Pushing aside a large rock that blocked much of the opening, the employee found a shaft that extended into the mountainside at a thirty degree angle. Using matches for light, he walked into the shaft for several yards until it became vertical. Peering down into the darkness of the tunnel, he spied a wooden ladder. Believing this to be a very old and long abandoned mine, and therefore unsafe, the employee returned to the entrance and shoved the rock back over the opening.

Later, it was learned that during the 1940s and 1950s a swarm of minor earthquakes generated a number of rockslides in the Tres Hermanas Mountains. One such slide covered one of the producing mines so effectively that it was never reopened. Though there is no way of knowing for certain, it is possible that the debris from a rockslide may have further covered the entrance to the San Miguel Mine.

The three treasure hunters who followed the directions in the old document to the specific locations in the Tres Hermanas Mountains reported they were convinced both treasures were still there, still hidden somewhere in the range.

As recently as the early 1990s, organized searches for both of these treasures were still being conducted, but to date no significant findings have been reported.

SIXTEEN BURRO LOADS OF GOLD

For a great many years, a large portion of the western United States consisting of what is now Texas, New Mexico, Arizona, California, Utah, and Colorado was ruled by Spain. The Spaniards, great explorers and conquerors, traveled to the New World for a number of reasons, among them to assess the strength of the native cultures and to inventory and extract precious metals they believed to exist in abundance. During this time, the Spanish government was deeply interested in filling its already substantial treasury and relied heavily on the expanding gold and silver mining activities in the western hemisphere to do just that.

Throughout much of the land they dominated in western North America, the Spanish operated dozens of rich mines and extracted thousands of pounds of gold and silver each year and fashioned the ore into easily transportable ingots. Once a significant amount of ore had been processed and accumulated at a mine site, it was loaded onto burros or mules and carried to governmental offices located in Mexico City where it was recorded, sent overland to ports on the Gulf of Mexico, and then shipped across the Atlantic Ocean to the motherland.

For many years, pack trains carrying millions of dollars

worth of gold and silver moved over dozens of trails, transporting great fortunes across the continent. The principal problems facing the Spaniards were the constant threat of hostile Indians and the often extreme aridity encountered in the expansive dry lands of the American Southwest.

It is an established fact that the Spanish discovered gold and silver in abundance in the mountains of southwestern New Mexico—the Datils, Magdalenas, Mogollons, Gilas, Mimbres, and Cooke's Range. Evidence for the existence of many of these early Spanish mines is abundant and clear.

In Grant County, such evidence is plentiful. Not far from the town of Santa Rita, one group of mines yielded millions of dollars worth of gold, and rich pack trains accompanied by a contingent of armed guards regularly departed this region bound for Mexico City.

Spanish rule eventually came to an end, but many of the Mexicans who worked in these mines continued to live in the region, mine the gold, and regularly transport it to the capital at Mexico City. Because the gold mines near Santa Rita were quite productive, a party of approximately one dozen miners and a supervisor remained in the area for eight months of the year. The supervisor, a widower who lived in a crudely constructed rock house with his ten year old son, kept the accounts and made critical engineering decisions relative to the excavation process.

The supervisor also decided when it was time to close the mine for the winter and return to Mexico. With the coming of the cold season when the frigid temperatures and snow descended on the valleys of the Mimbres Range, he would order the mine shut down, the smelted ingots loaded onto burros, and the entire group of workers to return to Mexico City where they would remain until the following spring.

One year as the winter snows were beginning to fall, the

supervisor decided it was time to leave. He ordered the laborers to pack the gold ingots into stout leather bags and prepare the horses and burros for departure the following morning. The next day when the sun was no more than an hour in the sky, the miners, led by the supervisor and his son, rode away leading the sixteen heavily laden burros. The journey began smoothly but little did the men realize that all but one of them would not live to see the sunset.

The slow-moving pack train meandered along the rough and rocky trail, passing through a valley which today contains the town of Bayard. At this point, the party headed due south, passing a low mountain known locally as Geronimo Peak. It was late afternoon, and the supervisor decided it would be prudent to halt early and set up camp. He knew of a fresh water spring south of the peak at a location called the Giant's Bathtub. The tub was a natural basin below a small waterfall; the tub caught and held spring water throughout most of the year and it was located near the end of the shallow arroyo along which the pack train traveled.

As the supervisor led the pack train to within twenty yards of the site, about thirty Indians charged from the concealment of a nearby low ridge and swooped down upon the unsuspecting travelers. Unprepared for the sudden attack, the miners were taken completely by surprise and, ill-equipped to defend themselves, were slaughtered by the merciless attackers within minutes.

During the first few seconds of the onslaught, the supervisor jerked his son from his pony and ordered him to hide in a nearby brush thicket. The lad quickly buried himself among the branches and, to his utter horror, watched the hideous massacre unfold before his eyes.

After removing the clothes and boots from the victims, the Indians then mutilated and scalped them. Following this, their attention became focused on the packs carried by the burros. It is not known what they perceived of the load of gold ingots, but the Indians generally cared little for the metal and were interested only in the animals. Curious, they examined the contents of each pack. Determining they contained nothing of importance, the Indians led the burros to a nearby deep rock crevice, removed the leather packs from the animals, and dropped them into the cleft. This done, they filled the crevice with rocks and debris collected from nearby. Finally, the Indians mounted and rode off toward the west, herding the burros ahead of them.

For a long time the young boy lay in hiding among the rocks, not certain it was safe to leave. All during the night he shivered in fright, and when the sun rose the next morning he crept into the open. Terrified and sickened at the sight of his mutilated father and the miners, the lad could think of nothing else to do but try to escape from the area as quickly as possible. Without a backward look, he began walking southwest along the trail, hoping it would eventually take him to Mexico City.

For many weeks the youngster traveled along the seldom-used road, covering the arid miles across barren expanses of desert. On several occasions he spotted Indians and he spent countless hours hiding in brush and among rocks until it was safe to continue. He found water at isolated springs and rain-filled potholes along the way. He subsisted on a diet of frogs, lizards, and cactus. His shoes wore out on the third day and he made the rest of the trip barefoot.

Miraculously, the boy survived the long, arduous trek. Gaunt and weak, he finally arrived in Mexico City and reported what had transpired in the remote hills near Santa Rita. To the best of his recollection, he sketched a map showing the location of the rock crevice where the sixteen burro loads of gold were dumped by the Indians.

Because of the fear the local officials had of the menac-
ing Indians, and because so many soldiers and miners had
been slain in recent months as a result of Apache depredations, the Mexican government refused to send an expedition into the region to retrieve the gold. The matter was
dropped and apparently soon forgotten.

The young boy who survived the Indian attack and the
long journey of hundreds of miles was sent to live with relatives. As he grew to manhood, he retained possession of
the map he drew, for he believed that someday he would be
able to return to the site and retrieve the incredible fortune in gold he knew to be hidden there.

The young man was never able to undertake the long
journey. He was forced to find work to make a living, and
he eventually took a wife and had several children and
lived the settled life of one who had many responsibilities.

But the lone survivor of the Indian massacre had his
dreams. Many times at night he would retrieve the crudely drawn map from the wooden chest where he kept his
few prized possessions. As he stared at it, he recalled the
death of his beloved father and the miners, murdered at
the hands of the Apaches. He remembered the dumping of
the sixteen burro loads of gold ingots into the rock crevice
opposite the bloody open space where the slaughter took
place. He often dreamed of the wealth that could be his if
only he were able to return to the site of the massacre.

Sadly, he would replace the map in the chest. As he
went to bed each night he prayed that one of his descendants might be able to take the map, return to the wild
and rugged country of southwestern New Mexico, and find
this fortune in gold.

*   *   *

Throughout its history, Santa Rita has always been a
mining town. Since the time of the early Spaniards who

dug the gold and silver out of the nearby mountains to the present when a large corporation extracts tons of copper each day from the extensive deposits found here, this area has known little else but mining.

Into this little community one afternoon in 1942 arrived a young native of Mexico. After checking into a hotel, he spent several days quietly searching the region on foot, arousing the interest and suspicion of many of the residents. Once in a while the Mexican would inquire about some particular landmark or forgotten trail as he pursued his search, but his English was poor and he often had difficulty communicating. Now and then, the newcomer was observed poring over an old, weathered map, one he withdrew from a leather case he carried.

One day the Mexican chanced to meet a young carpenter named Jim Bowman who could speak Spanish fluently. After several pleasant conversations with Bowman, the Mexican grew to trust him and told him the story of the sixteen burro loads of gold.

Bowman was intrigued by the tale but at first did not believe any of it until the Mexican showed him the ancient map. The young man told Bowman of how it had been handed down in his family for several generations until it had come to him. Finally convinced of the authenticity of the map and the tale, Bowman agreed to help the Mexican and together the two men searched for the treasure.

Much of the landscape of Grant County had changed dramatically since the days of the Spanish mining activity in the area. Interpreting the landmarks and directions on the old map were often difficult because roads and trails that existed over a century earlier were no longer evident, and in the quest to extract copper from the ground, the mining company had displaced and redistributed millions of tons of earth, altering the surrounding topography markedly.

As the two men worked intently at deciphering the old map, they were joined by another, a friend of Bowman's named Arthur Smith.

When Bowman and Smith were able to steal time away from their jobs, they would join the Mexican and spend hours searching among the hills and valleys near Hurley, not far from the southern end of Geronimo Peak. During this period the three became close friends and they often spoke of what they would do with the gold when they found it.

After several weeks of searching, however, the three men grew discouraged. While each believed in the truth of the tale, they were frustrated that their efforts had not brought them to the rock crevice filled with gold. Disheartened, the Mexican eventually bade his friends goodbye and returned to Mexico, taking the map with him. He was never seen again.

By 1946, Bowman took another job and moved away from the area. Smith retained an interest in the tale of the treasure along with a passion for finding it. He had studied the old map enough times to recall the directions and landmarks, and he searched for the lost rock crevice every chance he got.

Then, one day he found it.

After pinpointing a location he believed to be the site near the Giant's Bathtub where the miners were attacked by Indians, Smith came upon a wide rock crevice some fifty yards away. Peering within, he noted that it was partially filled with rock and rubble. He had no idea of the depth of this debris, but he was convinced the leather sacks filled with gold ingots lay just below.

On the following weekend, Smith returned to the site with his oldest son, Chester, and together the two men began removing a great quantity of rock and soil from the crevice. The work was hard and it wasn't long before they began to realize the magnitude of the task confronting them.

The two labored long, hard hours then returned home with plans to return the following weekend. Smith considered hiring some men to aid with the excavation of the rock, but felt it prudent to keep the location of the gold cache a secret between himself and his son.

The continued work of removing the heavy rocks was exhausting. Smith's job and family responsibilities often interrupted his quest to find the gold and he spent less and less time with the excavation. With his health gradually deteriorating, Smith was finally forced to give up the search altogether.

In January 1967, Chester Smith, now living in Portland, Oregon, told his younger brother, Calvin, about the sixteen burro loads of gold hidden in the rock crevice and the search he and his father had undertaken many years earlier. Calvin grew fascinated with the story and the possibility of becoming rich. Calvin nurtured a desire to travel to New Mexico and attempt to retrieve the gold.

The older brother had not lost his desire to find the gold, but his job kept him in Oregon. Enthused by Calvin's interest, however, Chester made plans to use his vacation time to travel to New Mexico with his brother and renew the search for the treasure. A few weeks later the two men arrived at Hurley and on the following morning went to the site of the rock crevice.

Chester and Calvin Smith were stunned to discover that the area adjacent to the Giant's Bathtub was owned by the Kennecott Copper Company and now private property. Entering the region at night so they wouldn't be observed, Chester led his brother directly to the crevice.

On arriving, they were disappointed to discover the mining company had constructed a road along the hill just above the site and in the process had pushed tons of rock and dirt into the crevice, covering it completely. The gold, easily worth several million dollars, was buried under tons of rock. Realizing their chances of retrieving the gold were virtually nonexistent, the brothers returned to Oregon.

In 1987, Chester and Calvin Smith decided to make another attempt at reaching the gold they were convinced lay at the bottom of the rock crevice, so they traveled back to New Mexico.

The copper mining company had almost completely changed the appearance of the area since the brothers' last visit twenty years earlier. A large earthen dam had been constructed at one end of the arroyo to hold back mine tailings, water, and other debris. The site of the rock crevice, already covered by tons of rubble from the road construction years earlier, was now under several feet of muck, according to Calvin Smith.

The younger Smith continues to believe in the existence of the treasure and remains convinced it still lies in the rock crevice. He is also realistic enough to understand that if there was any chance of retrieving it at all it would take a cooperative effort, involving high ranking officials of the mining company.

Chester Smith passed away in 1989, but younger brother Calvin is still hopeful that gold can be found. With the heavy earth-moving equipment owned by the mining company, he claims, it would be a relatively easy task to open the crevice and remove the gold.

His hardest job to date is convincing the mining company that the millions in gold to be found in the crevice would be worth the effort.

OPALS IN NEW MEXICO

The opal is a prized gemstone, and one of good quality will bring a great deal of money. This precious stone is formed at low temperatures from silica-bearing waters and can be found in fissures and cavities of rock of any type. According to gemologists, the finest opals in the world come from Australia. In the United States, Nevada has a reputation as a source of excellent opals, but elsewhere this beautiful stone remains somewhat rare for reasons that mystify geologists.

Particularly enticing to geologists, gemologists and miners of precious stones is the distinct possibility that a significant opal deposit might exist in southwestern New Mexico. Indeed, opals were mined in the Land of Enchantment in significant quantities during the 1870s. The evidence for this is abundant, but the actual location of the source continues to be a compelling mystery today.

* * *

During the 1870s, a party of four miners were prospecting for gold in the Animas Mountains in the southwestern corner of New Mexico several miles south of Lordsburg. Near the Animas Mountains, the borders of New Mexico and Arizona, along with those of the Mexican states of

Chihuahua and Sonora, come together. The region is arid, rugged, forbidding, and once served as an easily defensible location for hostile Apaches during the latter half of the nineteenth century.

In several places in this range, the prospectors found small veins of gold, but not enough to warrant a full scale mining operation. While exploring the various rock outcrops in the area, however, they accidentally discovered a deposit of opals. Enthused by their find, the men filed a claim and set about establishing a sophisticated mining operation.

Unfortunately for the miners, the Apaches resented their presence in the Animas Mountains. During this time, several different bands of Apaches roamed throughout New Mexico, Arizona, and Mexico conducting raids on small villages and ranches in the area. Following each raid, they retreated into the Animas Mountains where they felt safe from pursuit. Mining operations were often halted as the miners defended themselves against attacking Indians. After several weeks of constant harassment from the Indians, the opal miners finally quit the area and sold their claim to two men who expressed an interest in the gemstones.

By the time the two new owners arrived in the Animas Mountains several months later, they found they had the range to themselves since the Indians had recently fled into Mexico. Using directions provided by the sellers, the two newcomers easily located the opal deposit and proceeded to mine and accumulate the precious stones.

From time to time, the two miners would travel to Lordsburg, some sixty-five miles to the north where they would sell a few of the precious stones and purchase supplies. The two opal miners got along well with most of the townsfolk and generally stayed two to three days visiting with friends before heading back to their claim in the

Animas range. In conversations with some of the Lordsburg residents, the miners talked freely of their mine to the south and of the rich deposit of the opals.

For two years, the miners worked the claim, coming into Lordsburg approximately every two or three months to sell a few stones and purchase food and equipment. They once told the postmaster that it was their intention to work on their claim for another few months, take their accumulated stones to St. Louis, sell them at a high price, and retire to a life of luxury. When asked how many stones they had accumulated, the two men replied that it would take two stout mules to transport them all. Furthermore, they claimed, they would be leaving more than ten times that amount of opals still in the ground, still waiting to be mined.

When the miners failed to appear in Lordsburg for one of their regular visits, the townspeople and merchants simply assumed they had loaded up their cache of opals and departed the area, bound for St. Louis.

Sometime during the autumn of 1880, a commercial hunting and trapping party from Lordsburg entered the Animas range. On the second day of the hunt, they came upon the long-dead and desiccated bodies of the two opal miners. The unfortunate men were apparently victims of an Indian attack. In the pockets of their rotted clothes, the hunters found a handful of high-quality opals. For the next two days, the hunters, who knew about the existence of the opal mine in the region, searched for the source of the precious stones in the vicinity of the bodies, but were unable to locate anything. Subsequent trips to the Animas Mountains by interested parties also failed to find the opal mine.

Treasure hunters knowledgeable about the lost opal mine in the Animas Mountains of southwestern New Mexico continue to come to this remote location and search for the old mine. To this day, the deposit of opals continues to elude all, and the location of these precious stones remains one of New Mexico's foremost treasure mysteries.

HIDALGO COUNTY
LOST SPANISH GOLD CACHE

During the 1930s, Hidalgo County, located in the extreme southwestern corner of New Mexico, was sparsely populated. The largest town was Lordsburg, a city which owed its location and existence primarily to accommodating the railroad, but which also functioned as an important service center for the few miners and ranchers in the region.

Living in a run-down adobe house just outside the city limits of Lordsburg was an old man named Juan Ortega. Ortega, who was almost seventy years old, earned a meager living as a gatherer of firewood. Leading his old mule, Ortega would walk along the foothills of the low mountains near the town gathering wood and loading it onto the animal. Once the mule was burdened with all it could carry, Ortega would lead it into town and sell the wood. Living with Ortega was his daughter, Hortencia, a widow with no children. Hortencia cooked, cleaned, and cared for the old man.

Every morning after coffee, Ortega told his daughter where he would be gathering wood and about what time he would return home in the afternoon. One cool October morning he informed her he was going to Dogshead Peak to harvest some dead wood he found earlier in the week.

As Ortega picked up branches along an arroyo near Dogshead Peak, he spotted a bright reflection in the early morning sunlight just ahead. Adjacent to a rock outcrop, the old man found several gold coins lying in the sand of the arroyo. On investigating, he discovered a small opening in the exposed rock, one just barely large enough to insert his head. The coins, reasoned Ortega, had spilled out of the small opening.

Peering into the dark interior, Ortega saw several leather sacks stuffed into the tiny space. He reached in, pulled one out, and opened it up. To his amazement and delight, he discovered it was filled with several more of the same kinds of coins. Grabbing a handful of the gold pieces, Ortega stuffed them into the pocket of his ragged coat and hurried home to his daughter.

After showing the coins to Hortencia, Ortega told her he would return to the site the next day, retrieve all of the sacks of treasure, load them up on the mule, and return home. He told her they would soon be rich and the two spent the remainder of the day discussing how they would spend their newfound fortune.

The next morning, Ortega lashed a stout packsaddle to his mule and headed off in the direction of Dogshead Peak. Before leaving, he told Hortencia he would return home around noon.

By sundown, Ortega had not returned home and Hortencia was growing concerned. She walked for about a mile from the house along the trail she knew her father would be taking but could see no sign of him. Since there was nothing that could be done in the dark of night, she waited until dawn, walked into town, and told the sheriff her father had not returned from his wood gathering.

The sheriff, along with two deputies, set out in search of Juan Ortega. They had not been on the trail to Dogshead Peak long when they found the old man lying alongside the trail. The mule was grazing nearby. There was no sign of foul play and it was ultimately concluded that Juan Ortega had died of a heart attack on his way to gather firewood. On searching the pockets of the dead man's coat, the sheriff found the gold coins. Each was of Spanish origin, and each bore the date of 1738.

Later that same day, the sheriff asked Hortencia about the coins, and she related the discovery of the Spanish coin cache as her father had told it to her. For the next several days, the sheriff and his deputies searched the arroyos around Dogshead Peak for a small opening in some exposed rock but found nothing.

The story of Juan Ortega's discovery of the Spanish gold coins was soon widely disseminated throughout the area, and before long people arrived from as far away as El Paso, Texas, to search for the treasure. At times, the region around Dogshead Peak was swarming with hopeful treasure hunters, but all came away empty handed.

All that is known about the mysterious cache of gold Spanish coins near Dogshead Peak is what Juan Ortega related to his daughter. Their origin remains a mystery and their present hidden location continues to elude those who would search for them.

LOST SILVER LEDGE IN HILDALGO COUNTY

George Avery was a little known, small-time New Mexico outlaw who, while fleeing from law enforcement officers, stumbled onto an outcrop of rich silver deep in the mountains of southwestern New Mexico in what is now Hidalgo County.

Bad luck had plagued George Avery for most of his life, and it seemed like his situation was not about to change. While he and two partners were able to mine a quantity of the silver and sell it, his outlaw past finally caught up with him. He found it difficult to remain in the area and was forced to abandon his rich mine for a time. When he was finally presented with an opportunity to return, Avery was never able to find the mine, and its location remains a mystery to this day.

* * *

In 1888, Silver City was a bustling mining town with many of the city's businesses catering to the professional and recreational needs of the men who mined the silver from the nearby mountains as well as the owners of the mines who grew wealthy in the process. Like many such towns, Silver City attracted its share of salesmen, con artists, prostitutes, and drifters. One such drifter was a man named George Avery.

With no money in his pocket and having not eaten a meal in at least three days, Avery walked into a Silver City mercantile and, while holding the proprietor at gunpoint, robbed him of all the money in the cash register—a total of $116.00. As Avery fled, he was recognized by several people with whom he had become acquainted since arriving in town only days earlier.

From Silver City, Avery fled in a southwesterly direction through the Burro Mountains, eventually arriving at the town of Lordsburg, about forty miles away. After two days of hard riding through extremely rugged country, Avery decided to rest up in Lordsburg before crossing the border into Arizona, just a few miles to the west. He spent his first night sleeping on the platform at the railroad depot. When he awoke the following morning, he overheard the railroad clerk and the telegrapher discussing a recent message detailing the imminent arrival of Grant County Sheriff Harvey Whitehill and a posse of three men who were in pursuit of one George Avery for the Silver City robbery.

After hastily tying his bedroll onto his saddle, Avery mounted up and whipped his horse across the tracks and rode the southwest at full gallop. His intention was to stay off the main road and do his best to put as much distance as possible between him and the posse.

That evening, Avery set up camp near a spring at the base of a low mountain not far from the Arizona border. After unsaddling his horse, he brushed it down and turned it loose to graze on what available grasses it could find in the adjacent desert. Avery built a fire, cooked some bacon, and made some coffee. Weary from the long day of riding, he fell into a deep sleep.

Early the next morning, Avery climbed to the top of the mountain to see if he could spot any sign of pursuit. With a good view of his back trail, he saw no one and decided he had managed to elude Whitehill and his deputies.

Avery ate a leisurely breakfast, doused the campfire, and went in search of his horse which had wandered away. He found the animal about 100 yards from the camp, and as he walked toward it, he passed a curious looking outcrop at the base of the mountain. Peering closer, Avery quickly determined he had found a twenty-inch-thick vein of lead. Always in need of lead for fashioning bullets, Avery, using his scabbard knife, dug out several large chunks of the mineral and placed them in a pocket.

Before sunset, Avery crossed the border into Arizona, then turned northwest and rode for the mining town of Globe, about a week's ride away.

While in Globe, Avery, on a hunch, took his mineral samples to an assayer and was surprised to learn they were not lead, but a very high quality silver ore. Astounded at his strange luck, Avery began formulating plans to return to the mountain and undertake the mining of the silver. His better judgment, however, warned him that he was a wanted man in New Mexico and that he should allow some time to pass before returning. He decided to bide his time in Arizona.

During the next few weeks, Avery wandered over to Phoenix. One evening while playing cards at a local saloon, Avery met two men who, like himself, were small time outlaws on the run. During the course of the evening, Avery told his two new friends about the silver he discovered back in New Mexico. Throughout the night, the three made plans to sneak back into the area and conduct a clandestine mining operation.

Before leaving Phoenix, Avery and his companions purchased the necessary mining supplies. On the morning of departure, they stole twenty mules and herded them away toward the east and the remote mountains of western

Hidalgo County, New Mexico.

The three outlaws rode straight to Avery's former camp-site and set up a new one. A few dozen yards away they found the ledge of silver and immediately began digging it out, eventually creating a wide shaft during the next few weeks that extended approximately twenty feet into the mountain. As they excavated the ore, the vein grew thicker, promising a very rich deposit indeed.

Within a few weeks, the three men had dug out more silver ore than their twenty mules could transport. After loading as much ore as possible into leather packs and tying them onto the stout animals, they made the long trip to Globe where they sold the silver to a smelter.

With their new-found wealth, the three partners threw a party in one of the town's taverns, buying drinks for any and all present. During the celebration, the Globe marshal recognized Avery's partners and recalled that they were wanted. After gathering some reinforcements, the marshal strode back into the tavern and placed the two men under arrest. The response of the two outlaws was to draw their pistols and attempt to shoot it out with the officers. One of them was killed instantly and the other severely wounded. Avery had the good sense to keep a low profile during the melee and was not recognized by anyone. Two days later, the second partner died from his wound while in the Globe jail.

At the first opportunity, Avery fled Globe and returned to Phoenix. Believing he was safe there, he spent his money freely, living high, and boasting of his silver mine in New Mexico. Word of the free-spending stranger soon reached Phoenix City Marshal Henry Garfias. After investigating, Garfias discovered there was a $1,000 reward for Avery for the Silver City holdup.

Avery was promptly arrested, and while Garfias was negotiating with New Mexico authorities for his extradition, the outlaw managed to escape.

George Avery needed to get out of Arizona as quickly as possible. Using an alias, he purchased a railroad ticket and traveled to Yuma. From there, he crossed over into California, eventually settling in a little mining town near the California-Mexico border. Here he remained for just over two years, all the while planning a return to Hidalgo County and to his silver mine.

*   *   *

During the spring of 1892, George Avery, using the alias of George Anderson, returned to Lordsburg, New Mexico, and filed a mining claim at the county courthouse. This done, he purchased mining equipment and supplies and headed into the mountains to the southwest to renew his excavation activities.

On arriving at what he presumed was the correct destination, Avery looked around for his old campsite, but could not find it. Nor could he find the spring. For the next two days he rode up and down the flank of the mountain trying to determine the location of the camp. Eventually, he decided he was searching at the wrong mountain.

For reasons that remain unclear, Avery apparently became lost and disoriented on returning the small range of scattered low mountains, and they were all beginning to look the same to him. He searched for two weeks but could find neither his old campsite nor the silver mine. Frustrated, he returned to Lordsburg where he took lodging.

For the next several months, Avery made periodic trips into the mountains in search of his silver mine but with no success. Eventually, he left Lordsburg and for the next few years traveled around Arizona, living at times in Tucson, Nogales, Bisbee, and Thatcher. From time to time he would return to Hidalgo County to look for his mine but always came away disheartened and dispirited.

George Avery passed away in 1916 in Arizona. He died penniless and without ever relocating his lost silver mine.

*   *   *

The story of George Avery's Lost Hidalgo County silver mine has been handed down over the generations and periodically hopeful miners and prospectors come to the area in search of it. Though the exact location is controversial and shrouded in mystery, most researchers are convinced it lies somewhere along one side of Bear Mountain. Other deposits of silver have been found nearby, but none of them equaling the size and richness of the one discovered by George Avery.

THE AUTHOR

W. C. Jameson is a professional treasure hunter and an award-winning author of more than thirty-five books.

Other Books about Colorado
From CAXTON PRESS

Colorado Treasure Tales
ISBN 0-87004-402-8

6x9, 208 pages, paper $13.95

Jeep Trails to Colorado Ghost Towns
ISBN 0-87004-021-9

8 1/4x5 1/2, 105 photographs, endsheet map,
245 pages, paper, $12.95

Ghost Towns of the Colorado Rockies
ISBN 0-87004-342-0

6x9, 401 pages, 136 photos, paper $17.95

Pioneers of the Colorado Parks
ISBN 0-87004-381-1

6x9, 276 pages, 45 illustrations, 4 maps, paper $17.95

From the Grave: A Roadside Guide
to Colorado's Pioneer Cemeteries
ISBN 0-87004-386-2 (paper) $24.95
ISBN 0-87004-390-0 (cloth) $34.95

6x9, 500 pages, 100 illustrations, maps

Colorado Ghost Towns
Past and Present
ISBN 0-87004-218-1

6x9, 322 pages, 140 illustrations, map, paper $14.95

For a free Caxton catalog write to:

CAXTON PRESS
312 Main Street
Caldwell, ID 83605-3299

or

Visit our Internet Website:

www.caxtonpress.com

Caxton Press is a division of The CAXTON PRINTERS, Ltd.